Words o

Illustrations: Paching Hoé Lambaiho
Cover Illustration: Paching Hoé Lambaiho
Cover Design: Paching Hoé Lambaiho & Marie Chieze

Words of the Shaman

50 Quotes from
Paching Hoé Lambaiho

interpreted by a Psychiatrist

Marie Chieze

Book I: Consciousness

Illustrations by Paching Hoé Lambaiho

Edition 2024

Doubt everything you believe and seek,

that is where the truth lies.

TABLE OF CONTENTS

Introduction

When I first meet Paching Hoé Lambaiho[1], I am 34 years old. I am a psychiatrist, attending physician, and a researcher at the University Hospitals of Geneva. I have a solid background in psychotherapy, Jungian psychoanalysis, and philosophy. A question has haunted me daily for over ten years: "What is the meaning of my life?" This constant uncertainty prevented me from finding true satisfaction and authentic happiness in my achievements.

I have long searched for answers, explored numerous sources in search of light, in the writings of spiritual masters, and with mentors who could illuminate my questions. This vital aspiration only intensified my malaise, which grew over the years. At our first meeting, I was at the end of my strength, exhausted, on the verge of collapse.

Paching Hoé answered my existential question with a simplicity that unsettled me:

"Your mission, as an incarnation of your soul on this earth, is to leave this life having progressed, to become a better person, to get closer to your Creator. This is what we call the Evolution of Consciousness.

You are not sick. Look at your reality, and get up. Measure what you have accomplished, smile at life, be proud of yourself, of what you have done, and do not fear what you have yet to achieve."

These clear words resonated within me like a revelation, a beam of light dispelling the darkness.

The reality of my existence became simple. The partial answers I had accumulated over the years suddenly seemed to form a coherent picture. The pieces of the puzzle fit together, drawing a complete

---

1   Commonly referred to as "Paching Hoé" for simplicity.

9

image. The meaning of my life was a journey toward a deeper understanding of myself and the world.

Every struggle, every challenge on this path transformed into an opportunity for growth, giving new meaning to the relentless quest for improvement. Persevering was worthwhile because these trials allowed me to grow, to shape my life in the image of my aspirations. This perspective brought me peace. Viewing existence as an experience to become a better person led me to a sense of lasting serenity and contentment. I realized that happiness is not an innate state or a distant destination, but a will that is created through work on myself, my beliefs, my relationships with others, and my interaction with the world.

This first teaching from Paching Hoé awakened my curiosity. I felt the need to delve deeper into the complementarity of our two worlds: shamanism, based on spirituality and ancient wisdom, and the modern sciences from which I came. I felt capable of understanding his teachings and the scope of his knowledge. Together, we began to weave the threads of a dialogue between "the world of psy—"[2] and ancient wisdom, exploring how each perspective could enrich and illuminate the other.

Over the next two and a half years, I attended numerous sessions with both patients and students. I observed how Paching Hoé guides individuals on a path of inner liberation and introspection. I saw him use his knowledge to serve others, offering his support unreservedly. This generosity left a deep impression on me. Paching Hoé encourages everyone to embrace change, to become the active creator of their own life and happiness.

---

2   In this book, we will refer to "psy—" in a broad sense, encompassing professionals in mental health care: psychiatrists, psychologists, psychotherapists, psychoanalysts. The common characteristic of these professions is their knowledge of the psyche and the support of individuals, which is the aspect that interests us here.

This period of collaboration also revealed to me the similarities between the work of a "psy—" and that of Paching Hoé. Just like the "modern therapist," he seeks to heal the mind by exploring the depths of the human psyche.

Through a spiritual and psychological approach, he engages in a process of healing and awakening, helping individuals navigate their inner worlds to discover and activate their potential for transformation. This convergence between our disciplines highlights a principle stated by many traditions, from ancient spiritual philosophies to Jungian psychoanalysis: at the heart of our quest for well-being is the need for self-exploration and understanding, a journey we undertake together, guided by wisdom and compassion.

In exploring the links between shamanism and the "world of psy—," I have often found that modern medicine and traditional approaches are perceived as distinct, opposing realms, rarely inclined to dialogue. It is common for adherents of one to be reluctant, even closed, to the other. My experience has taught me a different reality. The complementarity of these two disciplines is a strength. Far from being incompatible, they nourish each other, offering a holistic approach to health and well-being that embraces the mind, body, and soul. This synergy between ancient wisdom and modern science opens enriching paths of healing and personal growth, integrating all aspects of the human being in its quest for balance and harmony.

The collaboration with Paching Hoé also prompted me to reflect on the relevance of his knowledge and the urgency to share it. In today's world, where psychological and spiritual challenges abound, finding meaning in our existence has become an imperative quest. The pressures of our societies, global crises, and the general feeling of uncertainty, even insecurity, fuel a collective thirst for answers, spiritual connection, and inner peace. In this context, Paching Hoé's teachings provide essential support. His philosophy, easy to access, resonates with particular clarity today. It invites us to rethink our priorities, deepen our understanding of ourselves and the world around us, and embark on a journey of personal transformation that is both intimate and universal. These teachings help us face the challenges of this life, offering keys to unlock our potential for growth, harmony, and true happiness.

Through the sessions and teachings received, I discovered in Paching Hoé a personality both grounded in reality, pragmatic and visionary. His ability to navigate between the inner and outer worlds with equal ease testifies to a deep understanding of the human psyche, the collective unconscious, and the universal principles that underlie this world. His approach, imbued with empathy and a connection with the essence of being, invites a journey of personal discovery that is both liberating and transformative.

His teaching, centered on the evolution of consciousness as the essence of life, intertwines harmoniously with the principles of Jungian psychoanalysis, promoting an inner quest for self-understanding and personal fulfillment.
Sprinkled with reflections on suffering, healing, optimism, and truth, it offers unique perspectives on how we can navigate our lives with greater awareness, acceptance, and love. Paching Hoé sees in each individual an infinite potential for spiritual awakening and personal growth, urging everyone to look beyond their illusions and false beliefs to embrace a state of wholeness and inner peace.

His dialogue with modernity, without ever losing sight of ancestral teachings, makes him a bridge between ages, offering a path to healing that respects both the complexity of the modern mind and the timeless wisdom of ancient spiritual traditions. In Paching Hoé, we find not only a spiritual guide but also a true companion on our journey toward a deeper sense of meaning and a balanced existence.

This book aims to be a witness to a transformative journey. The objective is twofold: on the one hand, to explore and propose ways to apply Paching Hoé's teachings, aiming for inner healing, deep self-understanding, and authentic personal development. On the other hand, it seeks to highlight the link between shamanism, as practiced by Paching Hoé, and modern sciences. The shaman's discourse is corroborated by the teachings of spiritual traditions, psychology, psychoanalysis, and current medicine.

This complementarity beyond apparent differences illustrates the inner path that opens to each of us: finding balance, a fruitful dialogue with ourselves, and with the world around us. This book invites us to recognize and value our interdependence, reminding us that we have both the responsibility and the power to improve the world we live in, a world we must protect.

I am eager to share this knowledge with you, not only because it has represented a personal path of healing and liberation for me, but also because I am convinced that everyone, regardless of their quest —spiritual, therapeutic, or the desire to actively take control of their life—can benefit from it. These teachings offer keys to understanding and action, to rediscover our role as conscious actors in our lives and our environment.

Reading Advice
This book is the first volume of a trilogy dedicated to the teachings of Paching Hoé. I have developed this trilogy to capture the essence of his thought around a central theme: the evolution of consciousness. This evolution comprises three notable stages: consciousness, awakening, and ultimately achieving wholeness. Each

stage will be the subject of an entire volume. Considering consciousness as the cornerstone of the path leading to awakening and ultimately to wholeness, this book aims to guide the reader through the first steps of this inner journey. Becoming conscious means accepting to confront reality and its problems to initiate change. We cannot hope to change without first understanding what needs improvement.

The 50 quotes I have selected for this volume focus on this fundamental precept of Consciousness, articulated around four distinct but interconnected thematic axes:

1. Consciousness and Spirituality (1–14): This section lays the foundations of Paching Hoé's thought, with a particular emphasis on understanding spirituality and the unconscious. The first two quotes, in particular, establish the guiding thread of his entire teaching.

2. Meaning of Suffering and Healing (15–28): The second part seeks to shed light on the meaning of suffering and the paths to healing, exploring how we can transcend painful experiences to find resilience and renewal.

3. Inner Transformation (29–43): This section offers avenues to initiate the process of personal change and transformation.

4. Teaching and Guidance (44–50): We all start by being taught, first by our parents. Our personal journey benefits others and helps them advance more quickly on their own paths if we share our experiences and understandings with them. This is the principle of the therapist, the spiritual master, the shaman, and the parent. This section offers ways to develop a helpful and guiding attitude beneficial to those receiving it.

The book is presented in the form of short, independent texts, each introducing a quote from Paching Hoé as the title. The explanation of each quote is a reflection I offer, establishing a dialogue between Paching Hoé's thoughts and ancient spiritual traditions, psychology, psychoanalysis, and philosophy. For some quotes, I have added practical suggestions for applying these concepts in daily life.

Each quote is accompanied by an illustration inspired by ancient Egypt and created by Paching Hoé. These images, rich in symbols, are not merely decorative; they are an extension of the invitation to explore the depths of our being. Ancient Egypt, with its rich symbolism, continues to influence and fascinate, offering a powerful visual framework for the concepts discussed. These illustrations provide a glimpse into the impact of the collective unconscious: ancestral symbols remain universal, touching many individuals around the world, and carrying deep meaning within themselves.

To guide your reading, this book includes a glossary at the end. This tool provides definitions and explanations of key terms used throughout the pages, illuminating concepts that may seem obscure or introducing you to new ideas. The glossary is designed not only as an informative resource but also as an invitation to deeper exploration. It serves as a bridge to understanding the spiritual, psychological, and philosophical principles underlying Paching Hoé's quotes. By familiarizing yourself with these terms, you open the door to a more precise appreciation of their significance and application in your own life.

This is not a manual of ready-made answers. Each quote is not an absolute truth but an encouragement to reflect. Approaching the reading with an open mind and curiosity, ready to discover a new way of looking at life, will allow you to evaluate whether the proposed perspectives resonate with you, challenge you, or help you progress.

This book is an invitation to a journey: a journey toward increased consciousness, toward a deeper understanding of yourself and the universe. It is a path that, hopefully, will lead you to become a conscious and joyful actor in your own life, armed with the wisdom and compassion needed to navigate this complex world.

I encourage you to read not just with your mind, but with your entire being. Let Paching Hoé's words resonate within you, raise questions, awaken answers, or even provoke doubt. It is in this dynamic process of questioning and discovery that true awakening lies.

Do not feel constrained by the order of the quotes. The themes that touch you more directly today may be different tomorrow. Give yourself the freedom to explore according to the calls of your heart, knowing that each quote, each page, awaits you to offer its wisdom at the right moment. There is no preconceived path or uniform answer; there is your path, unique and personal, which unfolds through your interaction with these teachings.

Each concept explored is closely linked to a fundamental spiritual principle. Spirituality is sacred, accessible to all, without distinction. This accessibility is reflected in the simplicity of its form. While the message of each quote may seem simple, Paching Hoé's thoughts are generally profound, and their application in our lives proves complex. Significant and lasting changes require time and perseverance. But each step on this path, each moment of reflection, and each effort of practice bring us a little closer to transformation and awakening.

These spiritual concepts act like Russian dolls: the initial understanding of a quote reveals a first meaning, which then opens up to new dimensions of comprehension. Each level of interpretation enriches our perception, provoking resonances and various consequences on how we see ourselves and interact with the world around us. It is this layered depth, this nested complexity, that makes Paching Hoé's teachings so rich. A first reading might illuminate one aspect of your life, while revisiting the same concept at another point in your journey might shed light on entirely different facets of your being or your relationship with the world. This multidimensional aspect of the quotes is not an obstacle but an invitation to continually explore, to remain in a posture of continuous learning. It is a call to fully embrace the path of spirituality, not as the quest for a definitive and immutable truth, but as an endless exploration of the infinite richness of consciousness.

To conclude this introduction, I return to the very essence of our journey: the hope and infinite potential for transformation that await us. My encounter with Paching Hoé represents not just a turning point in my life; it is also a testament that the path to expanded consciousness and a fulfilled life is accessible to each of us.

By sharing these teachings that have guided me, this book aspires to be a light that illuminates your path. The knowledge of Paching Hoé, perceptible in the quotes and reflections shared here, are seeds of hope and transformation, ready to germinate in the fertile soil of those who wish.

It is not by chance that you hold this book in your hands. Like me, it may represent the beginning of an exploration, an inner journey toward a better understanding of yourself and your place in the world. Each quote, each concept, each illustration is not just a call to reflection but an encouragement to action, to become the conscious architect of your own life.

I invite you to dive into these pages with the enthusiasm and curiosity of an explorer in search of hidden treasures. May this book be your companion, your guide, and your challenge, urging you to question, to believe in your aspirations, and to act. Together, through the teachings of Paching Hoé, we can not only seek but also find; not only rediscover our true nature but also realize it. This journey is the beginning of a transformation, initiated by an awakening. It calls us to explore and grow, endlessly revealing new depths within ourselves and new possibilities in our lives.

"Spirituality rests on three cornerstones: the divine love of our Creator, unconditional, eternal, and unlimited; free will; and Eternity."

Spirituality, as taught by Paching Hoé, rests on three fundamental pillars: divine love, which is unconditional, eternal, and unlimited; free will; and the Eternity of the soul. These principles weave together a complex web, offering an enriching view of our spiritual reality and our relationship with the Divine. This approach reveals an innovative vision of our personal and spiritual development and the dynamics of our relationship with God. It emphasizes love, freedom, and the continuity of our spiritual journey beyond our earthly experience.

Unconditional Love: The Foundation of Our Relationship with the Divine

Divine love is unconditional, eternal, and unlimited, offering us a solid foundation for our spiritual security and self-acceptance. This love transcends human weaknesses and envelops us in total acceptance. However, Paching Hoé identifies a major challenge in the human perception of this love: the tendency to project our own qualities and weaknesses onto the Creator, which leads us to conceive of God through the lens of conditional "human" love. This projection results in feelings of fear, guilt, and the fear of being abandoned or punished. Truly accepting God's unconditional love is a step toward liberating ourselves from our fears, allowing us to cultivate an authentic and loving relationship with the Creator.

Practicing unconditional love requires acceptance, tolerance, the ability to understand, grant freedom, and integrate the notion of time as an essential element for the evolution of consciousness. From this perspective, perfection is what is useful and necessary, not what is pleasing or complete. Unconditional love is devoid of suffering, constraint, fear, judgment, sacrifice, and self-denial.

Free Will: An Invitation to Spiritual Freedom

Free will is a natural consequence of God's unconditional love. It highlights the freedom and trust that the Creator grants us. This fundamental freedom allows us to make our own choices, explore, make mistakes, and grow at our own pace, without fear of negative repercussions in our relationship with the Divine. For Paching Hoé, free will is the essence of divine love. There is no greater gift than freedom, indispensable to any realization or evolution of consciousness. This perspective encourages a different exploration of our faith and values and allows each individual to seek God and approach Him uniquely and personally, in a rich and diverse spiritual quest. We are the actors of our spiritual evolution and our relationship with God.

The Eternity of the Soul: The Condition for Fulfilled Spiritual Growth

Eternity is not just a simple promise of life after death. It gives us a vision beyond our earthly experience, essential for creating the best version of ourselves without time constraints. An infinite path of spiritual development, it offers us the freedom to progress and draw closer to our Creator, freely, patiently, confidently, and without fear. This vision of eternity invites reflection on the continuity of our spiritual existence and our aspiration for deeper harmony.

A Dynamic and Peaceful Relationship with the Divine

The integration of unconditional love, free will, and the eternity of the soul forges a conscious, peaceful relationship with God. This relationship is characterized by love, freedom of choice, and an uninterrupted quest for growth, prioritizing progress over perfection. It relies on the certainty of being unconditionally loved, the autonomy to chart our own path, and the vision of an existence that transcends the materiality of earthly life. Knowing that we grow at our own pace, under the benevolent and loving gaze of the

Creator, allows us to rediscover joy, confidence, and serenity in existence. Paching Hoé thus proposes a spirituality where the relationship with the Creator is celebrated as a path of spiritual growth, inviting us to consciously engage in a dialogue with the Divine.

"The Unconscious according to Paching Hoé"

1. The Vision of the Unconscious by Paching Hoé

For Paching Hoé, the unconscious is envisioned as a vast superior memory, archiving every moment of our lives, the history of humanity, and the universes since the dawn of creation, without distinction of quality, truth, or falsehood. The unconscious is described not as a collection of separate entities unique to each individual, but as a unified collective unconscious common to all humanity. It functions as a universal memory to which we are all connected and is the real link between each human being. It contains everything that has been experienced, thought, created, and then forgotten since the dawn of time. This memory is accessible to everyone and reveals the true human potential. This is one of the reasons why, when we aspire to projects, we do not concern ourselves with the means or the necessary knowledge to achieve them, because we consider that everything is available in the unconscious and will be revealed in action. Our real capabilities are hidden in our unconscious. At this stage, it is important to realize that the potential of every individual can only be revealed in "doing." Besides Action, which allows for the unveiling of unknown abilities and knowledge, the psychedelic experience aims to explore the unconscious as a source of knowledge.

This conception of the unconscious transforms our understanding of individual and collective psychic and spiritual dynamics. It reveals a deep interconnection between all human beings, refuting the idea of a real separation between us.

The collective unconscious is built through the accumulation of common and individual human experiences. From this unconscious memory arise the values and laws of this world. Overall, human beings, being connected to this collective memory, share similar ways of thinking and beliefs. We thus understand how values and laws, recognized by the majority—such as the law of the strongest—become dominant paradigms in our social interactions.

The notion of the collective unconscious draws its roots from spiritual traditions, psychoanalysis, and science. According to neuroscience, we consciously remember about 10% of our experiences. Paching Hoé adds that the remaining 90% are stored in a collective unconscious memory. This apparent forgetfulness is not a void, but rather a veil that hides the accumulated knowledge and experiences from our immediate consciousness. Paching Hoé emphasizes the accessibility of all recorded information that, paradoxically, we have relegated to oblivion. This notion is embodied by the maxim attributed to the Master, who says to his disciple: "I do not teach you, I help you remember." This phrase reveals that we are holders of hidden memory, and the reality of our potentiality is buried in our unconscious. We are far from knowing our true capabilities.

In psychoanalysis, Carl Gustav Jung conceives the unconscious in two parts: the personal unconscious, which contains memories and experiences specific to an individual, and the collective unconscious, a deeper layer shared by all humanity, containing universal archetypes that shape our behaviors and cultural symbols.

According to Jung, it is essential to bring to consciousness the elements that unconsciously influence us, as this work on ourselves allows for the integration of all facets that constitute our being. This process, called individuation, helps us realize our unique potential and live a more complete and authentic existence.

Similarly, the practices of Buddhist and Christian monks reveal a universal consciousness shared through principles of interconnection and interdependence. The practice of intercessory prayer, in particular, illustrates human solidarity based on the belief that our mutual well-being is interdependent.

Phenomena such as synchronicities or irrational fears show how, in daily life, thoughts and actions coincide between different people without prior communication, suggesting an underlying connection through the collective unconscious. For example, an instinctive fear of snakes in a child reflects a preprogrammed belief in the collective unconscious rather than a direct personal experience. On the other hand, the child will delight in the presence of a cat, even though the feline is the most formidable predator. This example highlights the irrationality of the unconscious. It often leads us to react inappropriately or disproportionately, based on inherited thoughts and beliefs rather than a rational assessment of the situation. Our lives are constantly influenced by this unconscious, without us having a clear perception of it. Instincts, some of our deepest desires, and our reactions are echoes of this universal memory.

Paching Hoé's teaching emphasizes the need to regain control over our unconscious to exercise our free will. It is by systematically questioning our thoughts and beliefs through dialogue with others that we can choose what we believe. When necessary, it is through sometimes painful experience that beliefs change. Overall, it is this work on ourselves that conditions the evolution of consciousness.

It is about ceasing to be subjected to beliefs we consider our own, which generate inner conflicts and are the source of our suffering, as they distance us from our essence, our true nature. These beliefs lead us to adopt an erroneous vision of ourselves, based on the false idea that our thoughts define us. We are not what we think or say, but what we do. Our perception of reality and our own history is filtered through these beliefs, tinting our experiences with interpretations that alter our self-image. According to our version of events, we see ourselves not as victims, but as culprits, responsible for the aggressive situations we have endured. We view ourselves as weak, impure, inconsistent—in short, as bad people. This is why, during his sessions, I often observe Paching Hoé addressing his patient in these terms: "Now that you have shared your experience with me, I will tell you the true story of you as a child." He revisits the objective facts of the patient's childhood and cleanses them of all erroneous and negative interpretations formulated by the child and later by the adult about themselves. This new version often shows a great disparity between the two narratives and helps to relieve the patient of guilt, restoring hope and better self-esteem.

If we feel persistent suffering from which we cannot free ourselves, it is important to understand that the beliefs transmitted by our unconscious, especially those concerning our past, create erroneous perceptions about ourselves, distorting our interpretation of reality. Suffering does not stem so much from the painful events themselves, but from the erroneous interpretations we make of them, to our own detriment. This distortion between the reality of the facts and our interpretation traps us in a poor self-image, thereby increasing suffering. In such a situation, I recommend consulting a competent therapist who can help disentangle the facts from their interpretation and guide us toward a path of healing.

Understanding that we can choose what we believe and change erroneous interpretations about ourselves is essential in the healing process. Paching Hoé's vision enriches our understanding of the human mind, suffering, and our connection to each other. It challenges us to consciously navigate through this common memory to shape our reality meaningfully, recognizing our interdependence and reflecting on our individual and collective responsibility in choosing the beliefs and values we decide to reinforce.

2. Origin and Influence of Thoughts

For Paching Hoé, the collective unconscious constitutes the source from which all our thoughts arise. These thoughts do not result solely from our individual experiences but are largely influenced by resonances from the collective memory of humanity. His vision echoes Gandhi's warning: "Your beliefs create your thoughts, your thoughts become your words, your words become your actions, your actions become your habits, your habits become your values, your values create your destiny." Our deepest beliefs, often unconscious, shape our thoughts, which in turn, mold our words, actions, and ultimately, our reality.

According to Paching Hoé, our beliefs and thoughts are less the product of our immediate consciousness than a reflection of the collective unconscious, a reservoir of shared human values and experiences. This principle highlights the importance of becoming aware of our beliefs and thoughts to be able to decide our actions and create the reality we aspire to.

The Role of Free Will in Sorting Thoughts

In the face of this reality, Paching Hoé emphasizes the importance of free will in our interaction with these thoughts. Free will gives us the ability to observe and then sort our thoughts. This selection process is essential because it allows us to discern between thoughts that align with our true values and those that are simply reproductions of collective patterns. Paching Hoé's approach offers a structured methodology for this transformation journey.

Paching Hoé specifies that 95% of our thoughts are assumptions, unrelated to concrete and verified facts. These assumptions, if not examined, are taken as truths and can shape our reality inadequately, influencing our judgment about ourselves or others. The majority of these assumptions are to our disadvantage, resulting in a decrease in self-esteem and self-confidence. For Paching Hoé, personal development work requires meticulously scrutinizing our thoughts to distinguish those that align with our real aspirations and experiences from those that are mere erroneous or harmful conjectures.

I invite us to undertake personal reflection. Let's examine how many times we have doubted our own abilities to achieve a goal without taking the time to verify our experience or real skills. Think about how often we have questioned others' actions, attributing negative intentions to them without seeking to understand the reality or purity of their intentions. These negative thought patterns, if not examined, continue to direct our lives unconstructively. If we accept our thoughts as true without verifying them, we lose control of our lives.

A fundamental principle in spirituality emphasizes that we are not our thoughts. This concept is essential to initiate inner change. Buddhism teaches that attachment to our thoughts perpetuates suffering. Buddhist practices aim to observe, examine our thoughts, revealing their ephemeral and changing nature, and that they do not define who we are.

Similarly, mindfulness-based psychotherapies are based on this separation between our thoughts and our true nature. They teach us to observe thoughts without value judgment, to identify and challenge dysfunctional thought patterns, showing us that our thoughts are more frequently unfounded assumptions than facts. By modifying these thoughts, we change our emotional and behavioral reactions, freeing us from the grip of automatic and often destructive responses.

These approaches, both spiritual and therapeutic, converge toward the same aim: to free us from the influence of the unconscious, leading us toward a more conscious and balanced life. By practicing non-identification with our thoughts, we gain freedom and clarity, paving the way to a deeper understanding of our true nature and the world around us.

Paching Hoé reminds us that the unconscious, as a collective memory, does not integrate qualitative judgment; it archives truth and falsehood, good and bad, indistinctly. Although there is a correlation between our thoughts and our states of mind or the current circumstances of our lives, there is no direct link between what we think and who we are. This knowledge is liberating, as it frees us from guilt over our automatic thoughts, influenced by the collective unconscious and our environment.

Recognizing that we are not our thoughts is the first stage of the change process proposed by Paching Hoé. This selection process, based on the quality and verification of thoughts, allows us to determine whether they correspond to what we truly want to create and be, or if they distance us from it.

By adopting this approach, we engage in a process of cleaning our unconscious. By systematically rejecting any thought that is contrary to our true nature, that is not in line with our life experience, that distances us from our aims and the reality we want to create, we restore power to our immediate consciousness. This meticulous work of sorting and clarification is essential to initiate concrete and lasting change.

This approach, simple in itself, requires diligent practice and can be tedious. Nevertheless, it is essential to ensure that our unconscious is populated only with beliefs and thoughts that reinforce our true self and support our aspirations. By understanding that our thoughts are disconnected from our essence, we are equipped to lead a more authentic life aligned with our values.

By becoming aware of this reality and the influence of the unconscious, we decide to regain control, to think according to principles that reflect our identity and values.

3. Importance of Action for Change

Paching Hoé highlights an additional difficulty in this consciousness approach: true change does not come from reflection but from action. What we truly are is not manifested in our thoughts, often polluted by external elements or fear, but in our actions. Our reality is revealed through our actions and what we create. Reflection guides and prepares for change, but it is through action that our beliefs and thoughts are tested and their validity verified. It is the combination of this selection process and action that reveals our identity and reprograms our unconscious, thereby inducing lasting change.

Taking Action

Action allows us to test our beliefs in the real world, to see the consequences of our thoughts and behaviors. It is through the results of our actions that we can understand the direct causality between what we think and what follows. Paching Hoé emphasizes that the true potential of our essence can only be revealed through action. In other words, it is by putting our thoughts into practice that we can initiate concrete and lasting change in our lives and create the reality we aspire to.

Reprogramming the Unconscious through Action

Every action we undertake offers us the opportunity to reprogram our unconscious. The concrete results of these actions provide evidence that can confirm or refute our prior beliefs. If a new belief, stemming from the reformulation of a previous thought, is validated by experience, its significance is greater. It effectively replaces an old, unfounded belief, thereby causing a profound change in our way of thinking and acting.

Validation of New Beliefs

This process of validation through action is essential for authentic and lasting personal development. It is not just about changing thoughts or attitudes, but about testing these new perspectives in the real world. Actions are the true tests of theories; they reveal the substance and validity of our thoughts. By consciously choosing to act according to our new understandings, we actively forge a path that reflects our essence and highest values. This approach helps to create the being we aspire to become, transitioning from potentiality to realization.

Paching Hoé teaches us that true change begins with a careful examination of our thoughts and the conscious choice of those we want to materialize into actions. It then requires concrete and intentional actions. These actions are not just manifestations of our will; they are the foundations upon which personal change and spiritual growth are built.

This approach allows us to act, to create a reality that aligns with our needs, desires, and what we want to reveal. This cleansing reprograms our unconscious, replacing erroneous or unwanted beliefs with those verified by experience, which support our development and reflect our identity. By restoring power to our immediate consciousness and acting according to chosen and not imposed beliefs, we become the true creators of our lives, masters of our destiny, no longer victims of our unconscious programming.

4. The Process of Inner Change

Paching Hoé invites us to embark on a journey of personal transformation, which is at the heart of our evolution of consciousness. This process of inner change is not just a series of external behavioral modifications but a profound restructuring of the beliefs and thoughts that govern our actions.

Importance of Inner Change

Inner change is essential because it touches the very essence of who we are. Without a fundamental transformation in our way of thinking and perceiving the world, any external change remains temporary and superficial. Paching Hoé emphasizes that to live a fully conscious and authentic life, we must first undertake the process of sorting our thoughts and verifying them through experimentation in action.

A Continuous and Progressive Process

This transformation is not a single or rapid event; it is a continuous process that requires patience and perseverance. The path of inner change involves constant exploration of our motivations, fears, and desires. It often requires questioning and then reconstructing aspects of our personality that we had taken for granted.

Evolving toward Expanded Consciousness

By engaging in this process, we expand our consciousness, not only of ourselves but also of our relationship with the world. This expansion of consciousness leads to a richer life experience, where we are better equipped to face challenges, create meaningful relationships, and live in harmony with our values.

Becoming Active Agents in Our Lives

Ultimately, inner change makes us active agents in our own lives rather than passive spectators. We gain autonomy, deliberately choosing our paths and influencing our environment significantly. This process allows us to shape our destiny according to our aspirations and live in accordance with our true essence.

The process of inner change is an essential pillar for anyone seeking to live a full and conscious existence. It frees us from the automatisms and unconscious influences that dictate our behaviors and allows us to live with intention and authenticity. This inner journey is a path to greater peace, profound satisfaction, and lasting well-being. It also significantly contributes to the community and the world in general, as each conscious and balanced individual adds to the cohesion and health of society.

The Psy's Perspective

Let's pause for a few moments after these first two quotes from Paching Hoé, which essentially offer us the foundations of his teaching.

The first quote establishes the three pillars of spirituality— unconditional divine love, free will, and eternity. These principles provide us with a solid framework to understand the true intentions of our Creator, as well as our role and potential in the universe.

Paching Hoé's vision of the unconscious allows us to calmly build our own reality. We understand that we have all the necessary resources to freely and consciously create the reality we desire. With these two quotes as foundations, we have the key elements to begin our journey of personal realization.

Synthesis of the Unconscious According to Paching Hoé

Imagine a vast and imposing library symbolizing the collective unconscious. It is filled with endless shelves of books containing all of humanity's history and knowledge. At the center, a large, easily accessible display presents books that most people read, representing beliefs commonly adopted by the majority and practiced in society. These books are prominently displayed, reflecting their pervasive influence in our collective unconscious.

In contrast, the luminous principles that align with the Creator's intentions and our deep essence are subtly placed in less obvious corners of the library. These books are enveloped in a soft light, illustrating both their purity and difficulty of access. This light can be seen as a path which, although most aligned with who we are, is less traveled and harder to follow. It symbolizes the phrase: "The path of light is always the most demanding; otherwise, everyone would take it."

Visitors to the library are scattered throughout this immense hall. Some head toward the central display, attracted by the ease of access to these popular beliefs, while others, more adventurous or guided, explore the less illuminated areas to discover the luminous books that reveal the depth of our creative potential and the reality of our essence.

This image illustrates Paching Hoé's vision of the unconscious. It shows the dynamic between commonly accepted beliefs and the universal luminous truths that we constantly seek to discover, hidden deep within our unconscious. It visualizes the contrast between the easy, well-trodden path of popular beliefs and the less obvious but more rewarding path of beliefs that align with our deep nature. This image serves as a visual metaphor to explain the complexity of the collective unconscious, particularly the influence of immediately accessible beliefs that dictate our lives.

Complementarity Between Spirituality and Psychoanalysis

Paching Hoé teaches us that it is through spirituality that we can hope to surpass current knowledge about the unconscious and the psyche in general. Engaging in a dialogue between psychoanalysis and spirituality allows us to understand that, far from being opposed, these two fields are complementary and mutually enriching.

Spirituality reveals the Creator's thought. It illuminates our understanding of the psyche and our role in the universe and allows us to answer the question: "What is the purpose of my life?"

The Earthly Experience as a Playground

—Think of existence as a playground whose rules are not clearly understood without spiritual knowledge. Without these rules, we would act like players on a football field, unaware of the game's modalities and objectives. We would be limited, confused, frustrated, and disoriented about how to progress effectively.

Spiritual Principles as Guides

—The principles of unconditional divine love, free will, and eternity function as the rules of the game. They offer a framework and guidelines that help us understand how to interact with the world and ourselves more harmoniously and meaningfully.

—These principles allow us to see beyond immediate appearances, to understand deeper motives and purposes of our earthly experience.

The Unconscious as a Tool for Consciousness Evolution

—The unconscious is not just a passive receptacle of human experiences; it is the perfect tool for our consciousness evolution. We have within us all the knowledge available to choose and create the reality we desire.

—Through our free will, we explore, experiment, and test different beliefs and actions. Like the visitor in the library, we have the ability to consciously and freely choose which thoughts to read and follow, and which to ignore. We observe the consequences of these choices in our reality and adopt those that produce results most aligned with our aspirations.

Freedom and Conscious Creation

—By having access to the "entire library" of the unconscious, we have immense freedom to choose what we want to create in our existence. This library metaphor highlights the richness and diversity of the options available to us.

—This freedom reveals the Creator's benevolence, allowing us to realize our potential and play an active role in our own lives, at our own pace. For this freedom to be fully exercised, He created the unconscious, which can be perceived as a handicap, but in reality, it allows us to freely build our identity by cohabiting truth and falsehood, good and evil, beneficial and harmful. We are conscious actors and creators of our reality, in pursuit of freedom.

By understanding the pure intentions of our Creator and the tools at our disposal, such as the psyche, we can play with skill, conscience, and freedom. From this perspective, we can use everything given to us to explore, create, and live fully, being aware of our freedom and potential as spiritual beings engaged in a human experience.

The Process of Change According to Paching Hoé

To help apply this teaching in our daily lives, I propose a summary of the key steps in the transformation process as taught by Paching Hoé.

1. Examination of Thoughts

—Become fully aware of your daily thoughts. Pay attention to recurring thoughts and their nature—are they positive, negative, productive, destructive?

—Observe without judgment how these thoughts influence emotions, behaviors, and relationships. This awareness is essential as it is the starting point for any change.

2. Verification of Thoughts:

—Actively verify and critique thoughts: "Is this thought based on facts or is it an assumption?" "Does this thought serve me or limit me?"

—Determine their alignment with my values and aspirations.

3. Reformulation of Thoughts :

—Begin the transformation work by consciously choosing more positive, realistic, or useful thoughts.

—Clearly define what we wish to change or improve. Set specific goals for change that are both realistic and measurable. These goals should reflect not only our personal aspirations but also the person we aspire to become.

4. Initiation of Action :

—Take action, even small steps, to start materializing the desired changes. Action is essential as it allows us to test and adjust thoughts through practical experience.

5. Evaluation and Adjustment:

—Evaluate the consequences of the actions taken.

—Observe the impact of changes on our behavior and well-being, and the reactions of our environment.

—Adjust strategies based on the results obtained and feedback.

—Accept that a process of change and experimentation involves mistakes. Consider mistakes as opportunities to try another path.

6. Anchoring New Habits:

—Repeat positive actions to form new habits. Repetition is key to permanently anchoring changes in our lifestyle.

—Habits form the basis of our daily behavior and influence our thoughts and emotions.

7. Maintenance and Continuous Growth:

—Change is a continuous process. Maintain efforts and remain open to learning and continuous growth. This may require regularly revisiting previous steps to ensure we stay aligned with the initial goals.

8. Celebration of Successes:

—Take time to celebrate achievements, both small and large. Recognizing and celebrating progress is essential to maintain motivation and momentum throughout the change journey.

The process of change is not linear but dynamic. It requires time, patience, and persistent commitment. By following these steps, we make significant changes that reflect not only our personal aspirations but also a greater harmony with ourselves and others.

We will now delve deeper into this approach with the following quotes. Each quote offers specific insights into an aspect of these fundamental teachings and how they manifest in our daily lives, thus guiding us toward a richer understanding and more concrete application of Paching Hoé's wisdom.

"It is only through consciousness that we can hope to solve the ills of this world."

Paching Hoé's philosophy, grounded in optimism and a spiritual understanding of the world, offers us an encouraging vision to address and overcome the global challenges humanity faces. According to him, the transformation necessary to heal the ills of our world does not reside solely in technological or scientific advancements, but first and foremost in a profound evolution of our consciousness, both individually and collectively. He maintains that sustainable solutions emerge from an inner change that enriches our understanding and responsibility toward our planet and its inhabitants.

In the tradition of ancient Egypt, the maxim of Ptahotep, "Learn from the unlearned as well as from the learned," resonates with Paching Hoé's thinking. This maxim teaches us that every person, regardless of their level of education, holds potentially transformative knowledge. By cultivating an open mind and valuing the experiences of all individuals, we enrich our overall understanding and strengthen our collective capacity to initiate meaningful changes. This perspective is essential for developing elevated consciousness and pure intentions, the keystones of Paching Hoé's optimistic vision for a harmonious and sustainable future.

Paching Hoé emphasizes the importance of pure intention and collective consciousness in creating harmonious solutions. When the intentions of the majority focus on the protection and well-being of the Earth and its population, positive responses naturally manifest, resulting from our deep connection and interdependence with all that exists. This perspective is based on a spiritual vision in which the intention behind our actions attracts circumstances and innovations that reflect our noblest aspirations.

Paching Hoé views obstacles and suffering not as fated events but as opportunities for collective awakening and growth. Contemporary crises are seen as invitations to recognize our interdependence and progress toward higher consciousness. This optimistic approach transforms every difficulty, whether individual or collective, into an opportunity for learning, innovation, and improvement. Challenges become catalysts for our spiritual and material development.

This philosophy resonates throughout human history, marked by significant advances such as the abolition of slavery, the reduction of racism and armed conflicts, and the increase in freedoms. These progressions demonstrate our ability to surpass our current limitations and find innovative and peaceful solutions. These historical transformations attest to the impact of elevated collective consciousness and pure intention on the positive evolution of our world.

Paching Hoé encourages spiritual, conscious, and optimistic action, urging us to recognize the crucial importance of our consciousness and intentions in creating a better future. In the face of challenges, we have the choice to respond with hope, compassion, and a willingness to evolve. This philosophy not only calls us to reflect on our role in the world but also to act responsibly, guided by unwavering confidence in the potential for human growth and healing. The convergence of our sincere intentions, elevated consciousness, and lessons learned from human history illuminates the path toward a world imbued with harmony, peace, and mutual respect, embodying Paching Hoé's vision for an awakened humanity united in the pursuit of a sustainable and equitable future for all.

"To live consciously is also to foresee the consequences before any action."

Paching Hoé values the principle of living consciously and measuring responsibilities toward ourselves and others. He invites us to consider the impact of our actions before undertaking them, highlighting the inherent wisdom in a thoughtful existence. This way of living, centered on anticipation and reflection, is at the heart of the teachings of many spiritual and philosophical traditions, as well as psychological practices focused on awareness and mindfulness.

Living consciously means engaging in a continuous process of reflection, where each decision is made not lightly, but with a deep understanding of the potential repercussions. This involves heightened sensitivity to our environment, our relationships, and ourselves, recognizing that our actions have the power to shape our reality and that of others.

Acting and making decisions without considering their consequences can lead to a series of negative impacts on our psychological and emotional well-being. Failing to anticipate consequences can lead to feelings of fear, guilt, loss of self-confidence, and even deep inner suffering. These negative emotions and mental states underline the crucial importance of reflection and anticipation before acting.

Guilt is often the direct consequence of making hasty and thoughtless decisions that lead to undesirable results, especially when these actions harm others or cause us to act against our own values. This feeling is overwhelming, particularly when we recognize that the negative results could have been avoided with better preparation and anticipation. Realizing our role in these undesirable consequences can undermine our confidence in our judgment and decision-making abilities, making us hesitant to face future decisions for fear of repeating past mistakes.

This reluctance is often accompanied by a feeling that the world is against us, exacerbating isolation and pessimism. The aftermath of poorly conceived decisions can fuel this perception of adversity, intensifying our emotional distress and leaving us feeling constantly at odds, without support. This situation can lead to deep inner suffering, marked by regret, remorse, and severe self-criticism, potentially resulting in anxiety, depression, or other emotional disorders.

In addition to these internal effects, making thoughtless decisions can create a sense of loss of control over our own existence. Experiencing a succession of failures makes us feel powerless and unable to positively steer our lives. This sense of helplessness, combined with the fear of failure and unforeseen consequences, guilt, and regret, highlights the urgent need to adopt a more conscious and reflective approach to decision-making.

To mitigate these negative feelings and restore our well-being, it is essential to engage in deep reflection before making decisions. This includes considering the potential consequences for ourselves and others, seeking advice when necessary, and learning from our past mistakes.

Developing the ability to anticipate the outcomes of our actions and make informed choices significantly reduces fear and anxiety related to uncertainty, thus building a solid foundation for our mental and emotional health. By cultivating patience, reflection, and self-compassion, we strengthen our resilience, restore our self-confidence, and regain control over our lives, equipping ourselves with better tools to face adversity and progress constructively.

In the context of spirituality and shamanic traditions, this awareness is often associated with the notion of living in harmony with natural and universal laws. It involves recognizing that everything in the universe is interconnected, and that our thoughts, words, and actions resonate far beyond our personal sphere, influencing the very fabric of existence.

From a psychological standpoint, adopting a conscious stance promotes robust mental and emotional health. It enables individuals to navigate life with greater intentionality, reducing impulsive behaviors and automatic reactions that lead to negative consequences. By anticipating the effects of our actions, we become more adept at choosing paths that reflect our deepest values and highest aspirations.

Philosophically, living consciously confronts us with the importance of free will and self-determination. It reminds us that, despite external circumstances, we have the power to choose how we respond to life, how we act in our relationships, and how we contribute to the world around us. This way of living testifies to the human capacity to transcend automatism and rise to higher levels of understanding and engagement.

In conclusion, "Living consciously means seeing the consequences before any action" is a principle that guides us toward a more thoughtful and intentional existence. It encourages us to consider the impact of our actions with wisdom and compassion, paving the way for a life rooted in mindfulness and responsibility. Adopting this perspective is a powerful choice, a commitment to forge a future where every action aligns with our highest vision of who we are and who we wish to become.

I propose some key steps to practice this principle. When faced with an important decision, deep reflection before any action is essential. This involves taking the necessary time to evaluate all potential consequences of our decisions, not only for ourselves but also for others and our environment.

1. Pause and Reflect: Before making a decision, take a moment to pause. This allows for the mental space needed to assess the situation with more clarity and wisdom.

2. Gather Information: Collect all relevant information and consider different scenarios. A thorough understanding of the context and available options is essential.

3. Evaluate Consequences: Think about the immediate and long-term effects of any decision on yourself and others. Try to foresee both positive and negative repercussions.

4. Align with Values: Ensure that your choices are in harmony with your core principles and values. Decisions made in alignment with your deepest convictions are more likely to lead to satisfaction and personal integrity.

5. Consult and Share: Discuss your options with trusted individuals. Sharing perspectives can offer new insights and highlight aspects you may not have considered.

6. Listen to Intuition: Pay attention to your intuition. Often, our intuition guides us toward the right decision, especially when it's difficult.

7. Consider Impact on Others: Often, we forget to analyze the consequences of our choices for those around us. This lack of reflection can lead to misunderstandings, disappointments, and sometimes even conflicts.

Sharing decision-making with those involved not only prevents potential conflicts but also garners understanding and support from those concerned. This approach is not just ethical but a pragmatic strategy that strengthens relationships and improves the quality of our decisions.

8. Decide and Let Go: Once the decision is made, commit fully and let go of doubts and regrets. Letting go is crucial to moving forward without the weight of "what ifs."

9. Learn and Adapt: View each decision as an opportunity to learn. If the results are not as expected, take the time to reflect on what could be done differently in the future. Thus, we apply the principle: "I always win: either I win, or I learn."

By following these steps, we promote conscious decision-making, reducing the chances of regret, misunderstanding, conflict, and strengthening our self-confidence and inner peace.

"The aim cannot be perfection, but wholeness."

The quest for perfection, rooted in our cultures and psyches, juxtaposed with the wisdom proposed by Paching Hoé, who advocates wholeness as the ultimate aim, offers fertile ground for deep reflection on the directions of our lives and spiritual aspirations.

Origins and Evolution of the Concept of Perfection

Historically, perfection is an ideal that transcends cultures and eras. It finds its roots in ancient philosophies and religious doctrines, where perfection is often associated with virtue, moral, or spiritual excellence. In the modern world, this aspiration is amplified by demanding social and professional standards, erecting perfection as the ultimate symbol of success and achievement. This incessant quest for perfection, although driven by laudable intentions, turns out to be a chimera, generating frustration and a sense of failure in the face of an ideal that is constantly out of reach.

Perfection: A Societal Goal

Our modern society, with its ideals of success and excellence, conditions its members to aspire to a perfection often dictated by criteria external to themselves. This quest is presented as a promise of ultimate validation and satisfaction. It plunges us into a perpetual cycle of dissatisfaction and comparison, diverting our attention from the riches offered by our imperfections, true sources of authenticity and personal progress.

Perfectionism and Self-Esteem

The relentless pursuit of perfection reveals a lack of self-esteem, serving as a distraction to avoid facing our true internal challenges and preventing a realistic and compassionate assessment of ourselves. This strategy deters us from setting achievable goals that would allow us to create the best vision of ourselves. This quest turns into an unproductive cycle of external validation, amplifying our dissatisfaction and the feeling of never being good enough, thereby reducing our self-esteem.

Toward Authentic Personal Development
Recognizing this dynamic opens the way to authentic and rewarding personal development. Cultivating self-acceptance, valuing our progress and efforts, regardless of achieving perfection, allows us to steer our lives toward better self-esteem and a healthier balance.

Wholeness as a Liberating Path
In the face of the illusory quest for perfection, Paching Hoé's philosophy directs us toward wholeness, a state of acceptance and harmony with our being and life itself. This philosophy emphasizes the importance of embracing our imperfections, seeing our mistakes as learning opportunities, and celebrating our achievements for what they are worth. Wholeness is based on the conviction that our intrinsic value is not measured by our ability to achieve an ideal of perfection, but by our integrity, compassion, and capacity to love and be loved.

Wholeness in Spiritual Traditions
The philosophy of ancient Egypt and Buddhism each offer unique perspectives on the notion of wholeness compared to the quest for perfection. The Egyptian tradition values the importance of living in harmony with universal and immutable principles. The focus is on stability, social and personal harmony, and moral order as foundations of a fulfilling life. Buddhism, on the other hand, invites the acceptance of impermanence and the search for the middle path. This approach teaches that the quest for perfection is a source of suffering. Wholeness, in this perspective, is achieved through balance, a source of inner peace. These traditions offer a vision of wholeness as an alternative to perfection, encouraging a life aligned with deep values of wisdom, balance, and compassion.

Practical Applications of Wholeness
Adopting wholeness as a life guide involves accepting our limitations and recognizing our strengths. It teaches us the importance of valuing personal effort for its intrinsic merit, learning from each experience, and offering unconditional acceptance in our interactions, rejecting the unattainable ideal of perfection.

Embracing Wholeness for an Enriched Life
Paching Hoé's philosophy invites us to rethink our exhausting quest for perfection in favor of wholeness. It is a vibrant call to embrace a more authentic, balanced, and satisfying existence. This vision encourages us to reconsider our priorities, to free ourselves from the chains of self-judgment, and to celebrate our unique journey toward true self-acceptance. By preferring wholeness over perfection, we open ourselves to a life marked by compassion, harmony, and deep and lasting joy. This journey toward our true essence, nourished by discovery and acceptance, enriches our existence and illuminates our spiritual path.

"Truth is a belief among others."

The seemingly provocative proposition by Paching Hoé is nuanced by what he adds, drawing our attention: "with the exception of universal principles." This perspective invites us to question our convictions and embark on a continuous quest for knowledge. It reveals that our understanding of what we define as "true" is subject to change over time, influenced by advancements in knowledge, the evolution of societal consciousness, as well as cultural variations and dominant beliefs at different points in history, or simply by experience.

The fluidity of truth, its perpetual adaptation to new discoveries and shifting perspectives, underscores its ephemeral nature. Accepting this reality leads us to acknowledge that our current certainties may be challenged tomorrow.

This stance of continuous questioning is crucial for our intellectual and spiritual growth. It encourages us to remain open to exploring new ideas, to consider different perspectives, and to view truth as a journey rather than a destination. In this context, truth becomes a dynamic construct, reshaped by scientific advances, social movements, cultural evolutions, and the level of human consciousness, highlighting its inherently subjective and contextual nature.

However, mentioning universal principles introduces an important nuance, suggesting the existence of principles, values, or spiritual realities that, despite the constant flow of change, remain unchanging through time, providing an anchor in our relationship with God.

Exploring this idea through the teachings of ancient Egyptian philosophy greatly enriches our understanding of truth. In ancient Egypt, truth, embodied by the goddess Ma'at, symbolized order, balance, justice, and eternal truth—fundamental principles that govern the harmony of the cosmos, the gods, and humanity. This conception shows that, even though our human interpretations of truth may vary, the universe is structured by universal laws and immutable principles.

Egyptian philosophy reveals the importance of distinguishing between transient truths, shaped by our perceptions and context, and eternal truth, symbolized by Ma'at. This distinction encourages us to separate evolving knowledge from the fundamental truths that form the unshakable foundation of our existence.

The maxim of the wise Ptahotep, "One cannot attain the limits of art," offers a complementary perspective on our exploration of truth. In ancient Egypt, art was seen not only as an aesthetic expression but also as a means of accessing a deeper understanding of universal and spiritual realities. Ptahotep emphasizes the infinity of learning and artistic discovery, a metaphor for our eternal quest for truth. Just as the Egyptian artist continually explored new ways to represent and celebrate the Divine and the cosmic, we are invited to recognize that our understanding of truth is an ongoing process, always expanding and never complete. This maxim reminds us that, like art, truth transcends the limits of human perception and constantly challenges us to broaden our horizons and deepen our understanding of the world.

By embracing the principles of Egyptian philosophy, we discover that the quest for truth goes beyond mere intellectual acquisition to become a way of life aligned with universal harmony, justice, and balance. These eternal truths, which orchestrate cosmic order and our personal organization, invite us to live in accordance with realities that transcend our ephemeral understanding.

In conclusion, considering truth through the wisdom of Egypt offers us a more nuanced and enriched vision. It underscores that, even though our perceptions of truth may change, profound truths rooted in universal order remain. This expanded approach to the quest for knowledge encourages us to stay humble in the face of the universe's vastness while striving to align our lives with principles of justice, balance, and harmony that are both ancient and eternally current. This journey toward understanding truth, enriched by the Egyptian tradition, reminds us of the importance of recognizing the limits of our current convictions while pursuing alignment with the immutable laws that govern our reality.

"Freedom without individual responsibility, like freedom of speech without conscience, generates violence."

This statement by Paching Hoé leads us to reflect on the deeply interconnected nature of freedom and personal responsibility. This thought highlights the destructive potential of freedom practiced without the safeguard of responsibility and conscience, which can lead to chaos and violence.

In a world where individualism often prevails, freedom perceived as an inalienable right can become a vector of conflict in the absence of responsibility. This situation fuels hate speech and the spread of misinformation, underscoring the crucial importance of practicing freedom of expression with conscience and responsibility to preserve social harmony.

Examples of the Misuse of Freedom without Conscience:

—On social media and in the media: Unrestrained and limitless communication turns into a vehicle for anger and violence. Under the cover of anonymity, social media platforms become fertile grounds for misinformation, propaganda, and verbal violence. This underscores the need to implement rigorous controls and educate users about the impact of their words and shares online. As for the media in general, it is necessary to ensure freedom of expression while preserving social peace.

—In politics: Differences of opinion can lead to acts of violence, rejection of others, and disrespect for fundamental freedoms such as the right to move, work, study, and express one's opinions. These behaviors threaten the pillars of democracy and require a strong response to maintain respect and peaceful coexistence among citizens.

Individual responsibility, defined as the anticipated recognition of the consequences of our actions on ourselves and society, calls for an approach to freedom that enriches collective well-being through mutual respect and the preservation of social harmony.

To achieve this, educational, legislative, and community measures are essential:

—**Education and awareness:** Integrate courses on citizenship, ethics, and non-violent communication into school curricula from an early age. Teach the right to express different thoughts and opinions, and raise awareness that the limit of our freedom is determined by the freedom of others. Every individual has the fundamental right to live in peace and harmony. It is essential to teach our children that this way of thinking constitutes a form of intolerance and is synonymous with "the law of the strongest," which is the root of all conflicts.

—**Legislative frameworks:** Review freedom of speech laws to include safeguards against abuse while protecting fundamental rights. It may be time to reconsider the right to defame, humiliate, or offend others if we wish to live in peace with one another and evolve our society peacefully.

—**Community engagement:** Encourage open dialogue and public forums to share ideas and resolve conflicts peacefully.

—**Democratic institutions:** Strengthen democratic institutions to ensure that all voices are heard and respected.

The teachings of Ptahotep, a sage of ancient Egypt, resonate with Paching Hoé's approach. Ptahotep emphasizes the importance of wisdom, mutual respect, and moderation in speech and action. He highlights the pursuit of daily behavior that stems from the conscience of our deep interconnectedness with others and the universe. For Ptahotep, true freedom emerges not from the pursuit of our individual desires but from a life lived in accordance with ethical principles that promote balance and social justice. Commitment to these values is presented as the path to a fulfilling existence. Ptahotep's teachings guide us toward a life rooted in the recognition of our role within a broader social and universal fabric.

The perspectives of modern thinkers such as Amartya Sen and Martha Nussbaum enrich this reflection on the link between freedom and responsibility. According to Sen, freedom can only be fully realized if individuals have the necessary means to exercise this freedom responsibly. Similarly, Nussbaum emphasizes that freedom must be accompanied by social and ethical responsibilities to ensure true justice and equality. By adopting these perspectives, we recognize that individual freedom and collective responsibility are intrinsically linked and that promoting enlightened freedom requires social and political structures that support the well-being of all.

Ultimately, Paching Hoé's approach, aligned with these historical and modern perspectives, encourages us to reconsider our relationship with freedom. It highlights the central role of personal responsibility in the exercise of freedom. We are invited to adopt a conscious and enlightened freedom that not only respects the diversity of opinion and the well-being of others but also promotes constructive dialogue and peaceful coexistence. By adopting this path, we work toward the emergence of a society where mutual respect and social balance prevail, convinced that the most authentic expression of freedom is found in the harmony between individual freedom and collective conscience.

"The feminine and the masculine are equal in rights and complementary in abilities."

Paching Hoé leads us into a fundamental truth about human nature and the cosmic order, revealing the inseparable interdependence and complementarity between the feminine and the masculine. This vision is a call to transcend traditional beliefs that have often placed the masculine in a position of superiority over the feminine, to embrace a deeper and more balanced understanding of these essential energies.

At the intersection of psychoanalysis, philosophy, and spiritual traditions, the theory of complementarity, as developed by Carl Gustav Jung, offers us a framework to understand this dynamic. According to Jung, the feminine and the masculine, or anima and animus in his terminology, are present and operative in the psyche of every individual, regardless of their biological sex. This interrelationship underscores that unity and wholeness of being lie in the balance and harmonious integration of these aspects.

Ancient Egyptian wisdom, through the myth of Isis and Osiris, embodies this truth. Their story is not only one of eternal love but also an allegory of the necessity of the union of opposites for rebirth and the maintenance of universal balance. Similarly, the concepts of Yin and Yang in Chinese philosophy depict a worldview where the feminine and the masculine, though distinct, are deeply interconnected, their perpetual dance creating the fabric of reality.

This understanding not only illuminates the path to self-realization but also shapes our interactions with others. In relationships, whether in couples, families, or workplaces, recognizing and valuing the equality in rights and complementarity in abilities of the feminine and the masculine invites richer dialogue, more productive collaboration, and more empathetic connections. This leads to a rethinking of traditional dynamics, offering a living alternative to patriarchy by promoting a balance that honors and integrates everyone's qualities.

In practice, this vision transforms our approach to leadership, decision-making, and creativity. It encourages a more inclusive leadership where listening and intuition, often associated with the feminine, and decision and action, attributed to the masculine, balance to guide toward innovative and harmonious solutions. In the family sphere, this allows for an open education where children learn the value of equity, cooperation, and complementarity from an early age, laying the foundations for a more balanced society.

The convergence of Paching Hoé's principles, Jungian psychoanalysis, and Egyptian and Chinese wisdom leads us to profound reflection on the very nature of our reality. It reminds us that every individual, every relationship, every society thrives on the balance and harmony between the feminine and the masculine. It is in embracing this unity, in recognizing our interdependence, that lies the potential for healing, growth, and flourishing for all humanity.

"When I have too much, it means someone else is lacking."

Paching Hoé's quote sheds a bright light on the issue of equity and social justice in our world. This assertion confronts us with the reality of inequalities in the distribution of resources and goods, reminding us of the necessity of a collective conscience oriented toward equitable sharing.

This reflection invites us to contemplate the effects of our consumption and lifestyle choices on the community and the environment. It highlights the importance of solidarity and the intrinsic link between individual well-being and that of the community. In a world where the abundance of some can mean the deprivation of others, this phrase serves as a reminder of our shared responsibility for a more inclusive and just future.

From a psychoanalytic perspective, this awareness leads us to explore the shadowy areas of our psyche, those aspects we prefer to obscure. Carl Jung teaches us that integrating this shadow is essential for achieving psychic wholeness. Recognizing that our surplus can constitute a lack for others invites us to confront and reconcile these selfish aspects of our being, thereby contributing to our own individuation process while addressing social imbalances.

Spiritual and shamanic traditions, including ancient Egyptian wisdom, resonate with this idea. They remind us that we are all interconnected and that every action has repercussions beyond our immediate sphere. Universal harmony, as well as the order and justice symbolized by Ma'at, depend on our ability to maintain this delicate balance between giving and receiving.

In daily life, this thought urges us to reevaluate our relationship with possession, sharing, and solidarity. It encourages us to adopt lifestyles that not only respect the natural and social balance but actively contribute to the repair and healing of our world.

Consciously choosing to live more simply and in solidarity becomes a powerful act of personal and collective transformation.

In conclusion, Paching Hoé's vision transcends the critique of economic injustice to call for an awakening of conscience, compassion, and active engagement. It shows us that every decision made in a spirit of excessive abundance hides an opportunity for rebalancing, solidarity, and the manifestation of principles of equity and sharing. By embracing this vision, we work together for a humanity where prosperity is shared equitably, affirming our collective responsibility in creating a society where the abundance of a few no longer translates into the scarcity for others.

"Intuition is the 'higher intelligence': it never lies to us, it never makes mistakes."

Qualifying intuition as "higher intelligence" opens an intriguing window into human and spiritual understanding. Far from being limited to a simple instinctive reaction, intuition is presented as a privileged path to truth, an intrinsic ability to perceive and understand beyond the limits of analytical reasoning. According to Paching Hoé, intuition is the link that connects us to our higher mind, to our soul; intuition is pure and infallible. This approach highlights the contrast between intuitive knowledge and conventional methods of understanding, emphasizing the depth and reliability of intuition as a means of grasping realities that often elude us.

In certain contexts, intuition proves more effective than analytical reasoning due to its ability to quickly synthesize complex information, perceive non-obvious connections, and provide instant insights where rational analysis requires time and a methodical breakdown of facts. Here are some areas where intuition is particularly powerful:

1. Decision-making under pressure: When there is urgency or a lack of complete information, intuition allows for quick decision-making. Experienced professionals, such as firefighters or emergency doctors, often rely on their intuition to swiftly choose the best course of action in critical situations.

2. Creativity and innovation: Intuition plays a crucial role in creative processes. It helps make unexpected connections between seemingly unrelated ideas, leading to discoveries and innovations. Many scientists and artists report that their best ideas came to them intuitively rather than through strict analytical processes.

3. Interpersonal understanding: In social interactions, intuition helps read between the lines, interpret body language, and understand unspoken emotions. This intuitive sensitivity can lead to better empathy and more appropriate responses to others' needs, beyond what words can convey.

4. Pattern recognition: Intuition excels in recognizing patterns and detecting trends within large data sets, often without the individual being able to concretely explain how they arrived at a certain conclusion. This is useful in fields such as trading, management, risk analysis, business strategy, research, and medicine.

5. Navigating uncertainty: In the face of uncertainty and ambiguity, intuition allows for orientation when data is insufficient or contradictory. It can provide a "sense" or "direction" when logic alone goes in circles, guiding toward solutions that, while not guaranteed, often prove effective.

While intuition should not replace analytical reasoning, its use in complementing it enriches decision-making, problem-solving, and human understanding. Its conscious integration into our cognitive processes contributes to a more holistic and adaptable approach, capitalizing on the best of both worlds for optimal efficiency and comprehension.

In this panorama, intuition is recognized for its ability to reveal hidden truths, acting as a bridge between the conscious and the unconscious, the material and the spiritual. Psychoanalytic, spiritual, shamanic, and philosophical traditions converge in valuing intuition as a tool for knowledge and guidance, emphasizing its essential role in the human quest for meaning and truth. This universal perspective suggests that intuition transcends cultural and temporal barriers, connecting us to a wisdom and intelligence that surpass logical understanding.

The maxim of the Egyptian sage Ptahotep, "Follow your heart as long as you live," encourages listening to and trusting one's intuition for an authentic and fulfilling life. This intuition, considered as direct wisdom from the heart, guides decisions without relying entirely on reason. By following this inner guide, we maintain authenticity and balance between emotion and reason, fostering choices aligned with personal values. This approach enriches decision-making, especially in complex situations, and promotes deep personal development, leading to a fuller and more meaningful existence.

Paching Hoé invites us to reevaluate our own thinking and decision-making processes. He urges us to consider intuition not as a minor alternative to reason but as an essential component of our being, offering valuable and often more accurate instant understandings than those obtained through analysis alone. This recognition of intuition enriches our experience of the world, allowing us to navigate the complexities of existence with greater openness.

In summary, Paching Hoé's invitation to value and trust our intuition is a call to fully embrace our human potential. It encourages us to recognize intuition as a reliable guide in our quest for truth, reminding us that the answers to life's deepest questions reside in inner wisdom rather than in the external pursuit of knowledge. This approach resonates with a holistic vision of being, where intuition, thought, and action combine to form a path toward a more complete and enriching understanding of our world and ourselves.

"The unconscious hides our shadow, but also, and more importantly, the being we seek to create."

Paching Hoé's quote offers an enriched exploration of the dynamic between the shadow of the unconscious and the creative power that resides in each of us. This perspective integrates elements of psychoanalysis, spirituality, and philosophy to chart a path toward a profound understanding of ourselves, where personal challenges and dark aspects are not obstacles but sources of growth and transformation.

The Shadow and the Light of Our Being

At the heart of this reflection lies the notion of the shadow, described by Carl Gustav Jung, which represents the parts of ourselves we prefer to ignore or hide. Exploring the unconscious reveals not only our hidden or ignored fears and desires but also the innate ability to transcend these darknesses to unveil and create the being we wish to become. Confronting our shadow is thus seen not as an end in itself but as a necessary passage toward greater integration and authenticity.

Paching Hoé envisions the shadow as a whole composed of two distinct yet complementary elements: the dark part and the luminous part. The dark part contains our false beliefs, bad experiences, and false principles, which are generally shared by humanity. In contrast, the luminous part of our shadow reveals values, divine principles, and our potential. This duality between shadow and light creates inner conflict, thus stimulating the evolution of our consciousness to discover and fully embrace our human potential.

The Innate Creativity of Our Nature

Paching Hoé invites us to consider the unconscious not only as a place of shadow but above all as a fertile source of creative potential. This duality is the soil for deep personal transformation, where the individual becomes an actor in their own evolution, using their understanding and acceptance of self to actively forge their future.

Paching Hoé offers a vision of hope and liberation. Our false beliefs stem from the collective history of humanity; we are not directly responsible for them. Our true mission is to rediscover who we really are by freeing ourselves from the negative influences residing in the unconscious to fully awaken our consciousness. It is crucial to examine our beliefs, distinguishing those that align with universal principles and resonate with our deepest aspirations. We must choose to retain only the beliefs that bring us closer to the Creator's image of us, those that allow us to realize ourselves. By adopting this luminous vision of ourselves, we discover our essence, and by living according to these new convictions, we realize our full potential. Thus, we fulfill our soul's mission on Earth: to draw closer to the Creator.

Toward Personal and Collective Transformation
The practical implication of this new knowledge guides us toward a life where curiosity, openness, and self-compassion become powerful tools for healing and creation. It encourages us to embrace the complexity of our being, to value each experience as an opportunity for growth, and to consciously work toward realizing our potential.

Egyptian philosophy, particularly through the myth of Isis and Osiris, resonates with this vision, reminding us that harmony and wholeness arise from the acceptance and integration of polarities. Spiritual and shamanic traditions reinforce this idea, emphasizing our interconnectedness and shared responsibility in the quest for personal and collective balance.

Innovation and Contemporary Resonance

While rooted in a lineage of ancestral and psychoanalytic reflections, the way Paching Hoé articulates the "shadow-light" polarity brings a fresh and particularly relevant perspective to our time. By highlighting the active role we play in our own development, this thought opens innovative ways to navigate the complexities of modern existence, offering a framework for self-reflection and self-creation that deeply resonates with contemporary aspirations for authenticity and personal fulfillment.

Conclusion

This reflection reminds us that each individual carries within both the shadow of their beliefs and the luminous potential of their own creation. Recognizing and integrating these aspects is the key to advancing on the path of personal evolution, transforming challenges into opportunities for growth, and actively participating in sculpting our destiny. On this journey, we are both the artist and the material, shaping with courage and creativity the being we aspire to be.

"What is courage? Faith. The remedy for fear? Faith."

Paching Hoé offers us a reflection on the concepts of courage and fear, placing faith at the heart of our ability to face obstacles and navigate the uncertainty of existence. This perspective, both simple and transformative, resonates through different dimensions of human experience, inviting us to redefine our understanding of inner strength and how we can transcend our fears.

Revisiting the Nature of Courage

Traditionally perceived as bravery that defies danger, courage according to Paching Hoé is anchored in deep faith, a confidence that surpasses the conventional notion of bravery. This faith, not limited to a religious understanding, encompasses trust in ourselves, in the cosmic order, or in an ideal that guides our steps. It is this faith that allows us to remain steadfast in the face of adversity, nourished by the conviction that every trial carries within it the seeds of future growth.

Faith as the Antidote to Fear

Fear, often considered a paralyzing obstacle, is approached here as an emotion that can be tamed through faith. Rather than seeking to eradicate fear, Paching Hoé suggests embracing it, with faith as a companion on our journey. This faith offers a broader perspective, connecting us to a greater force capable of transforming our experience of fear into an opportunity for growth.

A Universal Resonance

Spiritual and shamanic traditions see faith as a sacred connection with the All, while Egyptian philosophy emphasizes faith in cosmic order and balance as foundations of harmony.

Applications in Daily Life

In everyday life, courage takes the form of a parent working hard to provide for their family, a student persevering in their studies despite difficulties, or someone standing up for a just cause. In each of these cases, it is faith—whether in themselves, the importance of their mission, or the future—that drives them to act courageously.

This quote invites us to adopt a stance of active faith. Whether in professional challenges, family commitments, or personal initiatives, it is faith in our values, our mission, and the future that inspires courageous actions. It encourages us to transcend fear not by denial but by confidence in the validity of our choices and our ability to positively influence our reality.

Conclusion

By integrating these perspectives, we uncover an enriched understanding of Paching Hoé's thought: true courage and overcoming fear lie in deep, multidimensional faith. This faith, far from being an abstraction, manifests concretely in our ability to act with heart and determination in the face of uncertainty. "What is courage? Faith. The remedy for fear? Faith." becomes a compass for our personal and collective journey, guiding us toward an existence where each step, supported by faith, is a stride toward our most authentic realization and our most sincere contribution to the world.

"God hides in the collective unconscious."

This quote from Paching Hoé should be seen more as an inquiry than a certainty. It suggests that through the collective unconscious, we become one with God, and His omnipresence is a powerful driver of our evolution.

Let's explore this idea through the concepts of psychoanalysis, particularly those developed by Carl Gustav Jung. Jung introduced the notion of the collective unconscious, which he described as a collection of beliefs, symbols, and archetypal motifs shared across cultures and epochs, constituting a sort of psychic heritage common to all humanity. Among these common motifs are spiritual and divine figures that appear in myths, dreams, and religions worldwide, suggesting that the quest for the Divine and spirituality is deeply rooted in the human psyche.

This interpretation does not reduce spirituality to mere creations of the human mind. On the contrary, it acknowledges its psychological depth and significance in our lives. The experience of the Divine, in its various cultural forms, emerges from the depths of the collective unconscious, where the universal motifs of our existence reside.

Universal Principles in the Collective Unconscious

From Paching Hoé's perspective, the collective unconscious contains the memory of humanity's experiences and beliefs, among which some are erroneous or limiting. However, it is also the seat of luminous universal principles, such as unconditional love, eternity, and free will. These principles, according to Paching Hoé, reflect the very essence of the Creator. Anchored in the collective unconscious, they resonate with the idea of a divine hidden in the heart of our collective psyche. Once recognized and integrated, they guide us toward a life in harmony with humanity's highest values: generosity, trust, self-respect, respect for others, and a sense of service.

Accessing the Hidden Knowledge of the Unconscious

This is a challenge explored by psychoanalysis, shamanism, and various spiritual traditions.

—**Psychoanalysis:** Sigmund Freud and Carl Jung proposed methods to explore the unconscious. Freud viewed dreams as a "royal road" to revealing repressed desires and used free association to bring unconscious thoughts to the surface. Jung, on the other hand, focused on the collective unconscious and universal archetypes, accessible through dream analysis and the individuation process, aiming to integrate the conscious and unconscious aspects of the personality.

—**Shamanism:** Shamanism uses trance states induced by rhythms, chants, or psychotropic plants to journey into spiritual worlds. Shamans consult spirits and guides to gain hidden knowledge and perform healing rituals to release emotional blockages. Vision quests, where the individual meditates alone in nature, are also common to reveal hidden aspects of ourselves. For Paching Hoé, accessing an "altered state of consciousness" allows travel into the collective unconscious.

—**Other Spiritual Traditions:** Meditation, like Vipassana or Zen meditation, and yoga, notably Kundalini yoga, aim to calm the mind and awaken latent energy within us. Mysticism, through states of ecstasy, seeks union with the Divine, revealing profound truths about ourselves and the universe.

—**The Importance of Experimentation According to Paching Hoé:** An essential method for accessing hidden knowledge in our unconscious, often overlooked, is the experimentation of what we do not know or cannot do. By daring to experience the unknown, we discover hidden knowledge and potential within us. This practice highlights our true potential, emphasizing the importance of action. As a spiritual master says: "I do not teach you; I help you remember." Through doing, we awaken the knowledge and skills buried in our unconscious, revealing our true essence and capabilities. These various approaches offer unique tools for a deep introspective journey, allowing access to hidden knowledge and integrating often unconscious aspects of our being.

Conclusion

With his intuition that "God hides in the collective unconscious", Paching Hoé invites us to explore the deeper dimensions of our being. By recognizing and integrating the luminous principles residing in our collective unconscious, we can overcome our shadow parts and limiting beliefs. This spiritual quest reconnects us with the highest aspects of our nature, such as generosity, trust, and a sense of service. By cultivating a conscious connection with these universal principles, we begin an inner transformation process. Thus, we can reflect in our daily lives the qualities of the Divine, such as love, freedom, and creativity. This approach opens us to a deeper understanding of spirituality, where God is an intimate presence embedded in the very essence of our collective and individual being.

"We distance ourselves from religion because the experience
with God is an individual experience."

This quote from Paching Hoé touches on the heart of modern spirituality and how individuals seek and experience their connection with the Divine. It suggests that a person's spiritual evolution sometimes diverges from institutional religious frameworks, pushing them toward a more personal and direct quest for the Divine.

This perspective reveals an understanding of the intimate and unique nature of the spiritual experience, in contrast to traditional religious practices, often characterized by collective rituals and shared, non-negotiable beliefs. The reality of God, being eternal, evolves in humans according to their level of consciousness. The experience with God that Paching Hoé refers to is profoundly personal and cannot be fully framed or mediated by external institutions.

In psychology, the importance of individual experience in the search for meaning and spiritual connection is well recognized. Individuals are increasingly seeking a spirituality that allows for autonomy, authenticity, and a personal exploration of the sacred. This individual journey toward the Divine can lead to a more flexible, adaptive spirituality that resonates with personal life experiences.

In shamanic and unconventional spiritual traditions, the connection with the Divine is seen as an inner journey, an exploration of consciousness that transcends the boundaries of institutionalized religions. These traditions emphasize the direct experience of the sacred, through meditation, spiritual journeys, or personalized rituals, highlighting the uniqueness of each spiritual path.

Philosophically, Paching Hoé's quote invites reflection on the distinction between faith and religiosity. It urges us to consider spirituality not only as a set of shared practices and beliefs but also as a personal quest for understanding and relationship with the Divine. This distinction underscores the importance of personal experience in the construction of faith and in how we live our spirituality.

The maxim of Ptahotep, "Art has no limit and no artist possesses perfection," sheds light on the individual spiritual experience. In ancient Egypt, art was not merely an aesthetic pursuit; it was intrinsically linked to spiritual search. Conceiving art as an exploration without limits resonates directly with the modern notion of personal spirituality that transcends traditional institutional structures. Just as no artist can achieve perfection, no spiritual experience can be fully framed by norms. Both domains encourage continuous personal exploration, where perfection is not a aim but an ever-moving horizon, prompting ongoing development and understanding.

In conclusion, Paching Hoé's reflection on the individual nature of the experience with God underscores a movement toward a more personal and introspective spirituality. It invites us to recognize and honor the diversity of spiritual paths, reminding us that the quest for connection with the Divine is deeply personal and cannot be fully defined by external frameworks. This perspective enriches our understanding of spirituality, encouraging us to seek and live our own spiritual truth with authenticity and openness.

"What is the point of suffering if, in the end, there is no light?"

Paching Hoé's quote, exploring suffering as a transformative path toward a deeper understanding of ourselves and the world, opens a rich dialogue between psychoanalysis, spirituality, and philosophy. This analysis offers a holistic perspective on the role of suffering in personal evolution and the search for meaning.

Suffering as a Universal and Transformative Phenomenon

Suffering, an inevitable and universal experience of human existence, is often perceived exclusively negatively. However, the vision proposed by Paching Hoé suggests that pain and trials have an intrinsic capacity to lead to "light"—a metaphor for wisdom, personal growth, or significant revelation. This perspective highlights suffering not as a dead end of despair but as a path of transformation.

Suffering Through the Lens of Psychoanalysis

Carl Jung's research reveals that suffering helps us grow on a personal level. It pushes us to confront what we hide or ignore about ourselves, promoting a journey toward a deeper understanding of our being. This process of reflection and introspection leads to inner evolution, allowing us to know ourselves better.

Spiritual and Traditional Teachings on Suffering

Spiritual and shamanic traditions present suffering as a central element of rites of passage and trials, using pain to access a new understanding of ourselves and the cosmos. This vision of suffering as an invitation to transcend the ego and connect to a greater reality reaffirms its role as a vehicle for spiritual transformation.

Philosophy and Growth Through Pain

In ancient Egypt, suffering was considered a necessary imbalance that stimulated reflection, questioning, and personal growth. Philosophy offers a view where suffering, though painful, encourages the acquisition of wisdom, compassion, and a heightened awareness of our shared humanity.

Contemporary and Personal Implications of Suffering
Recognizing the growth potential inherent in suffering invites us to adopt a more optimistic view of our trials. It encourages a courageous exploration of pain, not as an enemy to be avoided at all costs, but as an opportunity for learning and personal evolution.

Suffering as a Catalyst for Light
This quote reminds us that suffering, far from being merely an obstacle to our happiness, can be embraced as a crucial component of our spiritual and psychological development. "What's the point of suffering if, in the end, there is no light?" reminds us that it is in our darkest times that we can find the keys to unlock doors to higher consciousness, to a light that not only illuminates our path but also enriches our connection to the world. This understanding transforms our approach to suffering, revealing it as a necessary step on the journey to self-discovery and achieving a deeper harmony.

Can Suffering Lead to Light?
Suffering, whether physical or moral, can be seen as a powerful tool for consciousness evolution and personal growth. Here's how:

1. Awareness and Acceptance:
—Physical Suffering: Physical pain forces us to become aware of our bodies and their limits, promoting healthier living. Accepting pain as part of our experience develops resilience and patience.
—Moral Suffering: Emotional and psychological trials, such as loss or stress, push us to acknowledge and accept our deep feelings. This helps us develop a better understanding of ourselves and work on our vulnerabilities.

2. Developing Resilience:

—Physical Suffering: Going through physical challenges strengthens our mental resilience, teaching us to persevere despite pain and bodily limitations.

—Moral Suffering: Emotional challenges, like grief or anxiety, teach us to overcome psychological obstacles, strengthening our mental endurance and ability to face adversity.

3. Humility and Gratitude:

—Physical Suffering: Physical pain makes us more humble and grateful for moments of well-being, enlightening our view of life and helping us appreciate daily joys.

—Moral Suffering: Moral sufferings remind us of human fragility, prompting gratitude for positive relationships and experiences that enrich our lives.

4. Spirituality and Inner Connection:

—Physical Suffering: Physical pain can open the way to deeper spiritual reflection, prompting us to seek greater meaning in life and explore spiritual or meditative practices. It can also be a powerful reminder of our vulnerability and humanity.

—Moral Suffering: Emotional trials can push us to explore our inner world and seek deeper spiritual connections, helping us find comfort and meaning through practices like meditation, prayer, or contemplation.

5. Transformation and Personal Growth:

—Physical Suffering: Physical pain can catalyze personal change, pushing us to redefine our priorities and seek creative solutions to improve our quality of life.

—Moral Suffering: Difficult emotional experiences can make us more sensitive to others' suffering, enhancing our compassion and ability to help those in similar situations. They also push us to evolve and grow as individuals, learning valuable lessons from our trials.

Conclusion

Both physical and moral suffering impact our existence differently, but each can become a path to light by promoting awareness, resilience, humility, spirituality, and personal growth. Integrating these experiences helps us find deeper meaning and a richer understanding of ourselves and life, transforming suffering into a powerful tool for consciousness evolution. Overcoming suffering can lead to a state of peace and deeper understanding, integrating the spiritual aspect into our healing and growth journey.

"The painting on a wall does not speak to me about the wall,
but about the painter, just as your suffering does not speak
about you, but about the one who created it."

Paching Hoé invites us to reconsider our understanding of our suffering, both in how it is expressed and its origin. Just as a work of art reflects the essence of its creator rather than the nature of its canvas, our experiences of pain and suffering mirror the actions and intentions of others rather than our own identity or worth.

Art as a Mirror of the Creator

In art, every brushstroke, color choice, and texture conveys a part of the artist's soul. A painting on a wall tells us much about the person who painted it—their emotions, thoughts, and aspirations—transforming the wall into a space of personal expression. Similarly, our reactions, emotions, and suffering are influenced by the actions and decisions of others impacting our lives.

Suffering and Its Source

The comparison with personal suffering emphasizes the idea that we should not internalize pain as a reflection of our own fault or inadequacy.

Suffering results from the actions, words, or neglect of others, as well as from a misinterpretation of facts. Recognizing this does not mean rejecting all personal responsibility, but rather understanding that our pain is not an indicator of our worth or failure. The personality formed in response to aggressions and wounds suffered does not reveal our true nature. This understanding allows us to remove any guilt. Then, it is up to us to begin an internal change process to express who we truly are. This is where our responsibility lies.

Practical Examples

In daily life, this quote guides us to navigate our relationships more healthily. For example, if someone hurts us with their words or actions, it is helpful to remember that the pain felt reflects more the struggles or weaknesses of the one who hurts us than our own worth. This perspective helps us understand, let go, and move forward with a deeper understanding of the complex nature of human suffering.

In the same example, the quote helps us understand our reaction to the hurt caused by others. An excessive or intense reaction results from past conditioning and sufferings. It does not define our true identity. Understanding this distinction is crucial: it allows us to maintain intact self-esteem and focus on changing these behaviors rather than feeling guilty. Recognizing that our reactions are echoes of past pain helps us detach from these behaviors and actively work to respond more measuredly and consciously in the future.

Conclusion

Paching Hoé teaches us the importance of distinguishing between the source of our suffering and our identity. By recognizing that our pain reflects the aggressions or mistakes of others, we can begin the healing process with a clearer perspective on ourselves and others. This awareness allows us to cultivate compassion and empathy, both for ourselves and for those around us, paving the way for a more balanced and fulfilling life.

"It is when the child discovers the impermanence of life and death that the ego emerges."

This quote offers an original perspective on the development of individual consciousness, suggesting that it is through confronting the constant flow of changes, leading to the finiteness of existence, that the child begins to perceive themselves as a distinct entity, separate from the world around them.

From Unity to Individuality: Awakening to Self-Consciousness
Paching Hoé's thought draws on spiritual traditions, particularly Buddhism. The child initially lives in a state of unity with their environment. Their discovery of impermanence and death marks the beginning of self-consciousness as a separate entity. This realization, though unsettling, is crucial for the formation of the ego.

Psychology and Philosophy: Death as a Catalyst
The recognition of mortality, according to Carl Jung, is essential for self-realization and integral personal development. Friedrich Nietzsche and other philosophers have also explored how death serves as a stimulus to live fully and achieve our aspirations.

Development and Impermanence: Contemporary Perspectives
Research in developmental psychology shows that the understanding of death evolves with age and significantly affects the perception of self and the world. Although these studies do not establish a direct link between this awareness and the emergence of the ego, they indicate how the realization of impermanence shapes our identity construction.

The Utility of the Ego
The ego, self-awareness as a distinct entity, is indispensable in perceiving and interacting with the world. It acts as a personal prism that filters everything. It drives our aspiration for excellence, crucial for robust self-esteem, resilience, and confidence in our choices.

Without the ego, the quest for personal fulfillment and our ability to challenge ourselves would wither.

The Excess of Ego
An excess of ego distorts reality, leading to arrogance, difficulty in recognizing mistakes, and barriers to personal growth. Professionally, it undermines teamwork and leadership.

The Ego: Between Shadow and Light
The ego, in its duality, is both an obstacle and a necessary tool. Managing it well becomes an art: in excess, we lose our way; without ego, we lose our identity. The key is in seeking a balance that fosters personal fulfillment while maintaining an authentic connection with others.

Conclusion
The journey through understanding the ego, from its awakening to its role as a driver of our personal evolution, underscores the importance of finding balance. Paching Hoé's quote invites us to introspection: recognizing and accepting the ego while putting it in its place, to transform our awareness of finiteness into a catalyst for an authentic, ambitious, and fulfilling life. The ability to navigate between self-assertion and openness to others, between personal achievement and compassion, is essential for a thoughtful and enriched existence.

"We find wholeness in inner peace. Let us seek to make peace with our past, with those who have caused us pain, with our bad experiences, and with ourselves. Let us not leave this world without having found peace."

This quote from Paching Hoé offers a profound reflection on the path to inner wholeness through the pursuit of peace in various aspects of our lives.

Wholeness and Inner Peace

Paching Hoé first evokes the notion of "wholeness," a form of complete fulfillment and satisfaction of the being. This wholeness does not come from material wealth or external success, but rather from "inner peace." The author thus suggests that true wealth lies in peace of mind and inner harmony. This notion finds its roots in the spiritual traditions of ancient Egypt and Buddhism.

Making Peace with Our Past

Next, Paching Hoé invites us to "make peace with our past." This phrase resonates with the notion of resilience and emotional healing. We often carry burdens from the past that hinder our ability to be present. Making peace with our past involves accepting what has been, embracing our mistakes, and letting go of the resentments that hold us prisoner.

Forgiving Those Who Have Hurt Us

Paching Hoé also emphasizes the importance of making peace with those who have caused us pain. This process can be particularly difficult but is essential for our own well-being. By letting go of resentment and seeking to understand the reasons behind the actions that caused our suffering, we free ourselves from the toxic grip of bitterness and anger.

Accepting Our Negative Experiences

Moreover, the author invites us to make peace with our "bad experiences." This means accepting life's setbacks as opportunities for learning and growth. By recognizing the transformative power of challenges, we can transcend pain and discover a deeper meaning in our most difficult experiences.

Finding Peace with Ourselves

Finally, Paching Hoé challenges us to find peace with ourselves. This unconditional self-acceptance is the foundation of inner peace. By cultivating self-love and compassion, we can transcend our imperfections and embrace our authentic selves with kindness.

Conclusion

Paching Hoé's thoughts invite us to undertake an inner journey toward wholeness by making peace with our past, our relationships, our experiences, and ourselves. It is a powerful reminder of the importance of emotional healing and resilience in our quest for lasting happiness and fulfillment.

"Making peace with our past means choosing to take responsibility for what we experience."

Approaching peace with our past through the lens of personal responsibility opens up a rich panorama of possibilities for growth and awakening. Paching Hoé's quote invites us to explore how this inner reconciliation transforms our relationship with the world, others, and ourselves.

The Inner Journey Toward Responsibility

The invitation to make peace with our past is an inner journey that begins with the exploration of our own consciousness. This journey requires delving into the depths of our personal history, examining the choices made, the paths taken, and most importantly, the underlying motives that have guided our actions. This process of introspection is not only an act of courage but also a quest for truth about ourselves.

Transformation Through Acceptance

Accepting our past means recognizing and embracing all facets of our experience, including those that are difficult to admit. This acceptance does not imply passivity in the face of errors or endured pain but rather a willingness to understand their origins and actively transform their impact on our lives. It is through this approach that we truly reclaim our history, turning it into a source of strength and wisdom.

Responsibility as Liberation

Taking responsibility liberates us from the victim mentality and empowers us as active participants in our lives. This shift in perspective equips us to face future challenges with increased resilience and renewed clarity. In this context, responsibility is not a burden but a power: the power to choose how to respond to life's uncertainties, the power to find meaning in our suffering and to transcend it.

Reconciliation with Others and the Universe

Making peace with our past also means reexamining our relationships with others and the universe. By understanding and accepting our part in past dynamics, we pave the way for more authentic and harmonious relationships. This inner peace is then reflected in our interactions with the world, positively influencing our environment and contributing to a more serene collective consciousness.

The Role of Community and Sharing

The journey toward inner peace is deeply personal but also nourished by community and sharing. Spiritual and shamanic traditions often emphasize the role of community in the healing and transformation process. Sharing our stories, struggles, and victories becomes a source of inspiration and support for others, creating a virtuous cycle of growth and empathy.

An Invitation to Evolution

Paching Hoé's quote invites us to a profound reflection on the meaning of our existence and the power of personal responsibility in the quest for wholeness. By making peace with our past, we do not merely heal our wounds; we open the door to a continuous process of evolution, where each experience, good or bad, becomes an essential link in our development. This perspective encourages us to live with increased intentionality, aware of the impact of our choices and receptive to the beauty of personal transformation.

"Do not lament over your past, but rather look at the beauty of your future."

Paching Hoé's quote invites us to embrace life with a renewed perspective. It encourages not only transcending past regrets and disappointments but also opening our eyes to the infinite possibilities and promises that the future holds. Rooted in psychological, spiritual, and philosophical traditions, this thought sheds light on how we can navigate the waters of existence with enthusiasm and hope.

Toward a Future of Possibilities

The idea of looking to the future with hope opens up a horizon of limitless possibilities. This optimistic orientation toward the future encourages us to see it not as an immutable destiny but as a blank canvas ready to be adorned with the colors of our dreams and aspirations. Adopting a proactive approach to life engages us in actively building our future reality, using the lessons learned from the past to forge a future in harmony with our most authentic desires.

Reconciliation with the Past

Not lamenting over the past suggests a path toward healing and deep reconciliation with ourselves. It means welcoming and accepting our past experiences, whether they brought joy or pain, as integral parts of our current narrative. This process frees us from the bonds of regret and bitterness, creating the necessary space for newness and personal growth.

Hope as a Catalyst

Hope is essential as the driving force that propels us forward. Belief in a promising future lights our way through periods of uncertainty and challenges. Nurturing hope at the core of our lives is crucial for maintaining our drive toward achieving our aims and realizing our full potential.

Contributing to a Collective Future

Looking to the future with optimism is not only a personal benefit but also a collective one. By cultivating a positive vision of what lies ahead, we become sources of inspiration for those around us. Our aspiration for a better future motivates us to act constructively within our community and to work toward a world filled with peace, equity, and harmony.

A Smile Toward the Future

"Do not lament over your past, but rather look at the beauty of your future" is more than just an invitation to optimism; it is a call to positive action, to embrace the future with a smile. This philosophy encourages us to take control of our destiny, to turn our aspirations into concrete realities, and to welcome each day as a unique opportunity to chart our course toward a flourishing future. By adopting this perspective, we celebrate our individual journey while contributing to the creation of a radiant collective future marked by love, solidarity, and mutual progress. Paching Hoé, through this luminous expression of life, invites us to smile at the future, to smile at life itself.

"There is no greater illusion than recognizing ourselves in the eyes of another."

Paching Hoé offers a reflection on the construction of identity and the dangers of seeking validation and recognition in the eyes of others. This philosophy invites us to explore the depths of our being, distinguishing between the image of ourselves that others reflect back to us and our true essence, often hidden by societal expectations and judgments.

Identity and Illusion

The gaze of others is deceptive, urging us to shape our behavior, choices, and desires based on perceived norms and expectations. This quest for external approval is a source of vulnerability because it places our sense of worth and self-esteem in the hands of others. Paching Hoé highlights the necessity of detaching from this dependency, emphasizing that true self-understanding comes from within.

Creating a Persona to Please

The creation of a persona to gain others' approval is often motivated by low self-esteem and a deep desire to be loved and accepted. Although this strategy may offer temporary gratification, it is fundamentally fragile and unsustainable in the long term. It leads to a cycle of dependence where our well-being and self-perception fluctuate with the changing opinions of others.

Psychological Consequences

The gap between our true nature and the persona we project creates internal dissonance, leading to anxiety, depression, and a persistent sense of inauthenticity. The constant effort to maintain a pleasing façade to others depletes our emotional and mental resources, distancing us from the possibility of cultivating an authentic relationship with ourselves and others.

The Path to Authenticity

True healing and fulfillment require breaking the cycle of dependence on others' perceptions and rebuilding our self-esteem on more solid, personal foundations. This involves a complex journey of self-reflection, self-acceptance, and reconciliation with aspects of ourselves we have neglected or hidden. Freeing ourselves from the illusion of recognizing ourselves in others' eyes opens the way to a more authentic life, where our choices and identity are determined by our values, aspirations, and personal integrity.

Conclusion

Paching Hoé invites us to consider the quest for external approval as vain. This illusion distances us from our true essence. By turning away from the persona created to please and embracing authenticity, we discover deeper peace and satisfaction. We also open the possibility for more genuine and meaningful relationships. This perspective teaches us that true freedom lies in the ability to live in alignment with ourselves, independent of the gaze and judgments of others.

"How can you give to others what you do not know how to give
to yourself?"

This quote prompts introspection on the dynamics of self-love and altruism. Our ability to offer generosity, love, and support to others is intrinsically linked to our relationship with ourselves. This statement underscores the importance of self-compassion and inner well-being as prerequisites for genuine outward generosity.

Self-Love as the Foundation of Altruism

At the heart of this reflection lies the necessity of cultivating deep love and respect for ourselves. This involves a commitment to inner exploration and healing, recognizing our needs, limits, and aspirations. To love others fully and contribute positively to their lives, we must first love and accept ourselves unconditionally.

The Peril of Self-Neglect

Ignoring this fundamental principle leads to an exhausting or inauthentic form of altruism, where our actions toward others are motivated by the desire for external validation rather than true altruistic intent. This approach not only drains our vital energy but also risks building relationships based on dependency and the need for recognition, rather than on genuine mutual love and respect.

Authenticity and Genuine Presence

Practicing self-compassion and self-love allows us to develop an authentic presence and a nurturing space for others. By being at peace with ourselves, we can offer real support and be truly present for those around us. Self-compassion teaches us patience, understanding, and kindness, qualities that we can then extend to others more naturally and effectively.

Interdependence of Self-Care and Caring for Others

Paching Hoé also highlights the interconnection between self-care and caring for others. In many spiritual, psychological, and philosophical traditions, this balance between attention to ourselves and to others is considered essential for achieving overall harmony and fulfillment. By nourishing ourselves, we accumulate the resources necessary to nourish others, thus creating a virtuous cycle of well-being and generosity.

Toward a Harmonious Balance

The question posed by Paching Hoé encourages us to embark on an inner journey toward self-acceptance and self-love, recognizing that this personal journey is inextricably linked to our capacity to do good around us. By cultivating a loving and compassionate relationship with ourselves, we become better equipped to offer these same qualities to the world. This realization opens up a liberating perspective, reminding us that the foundation of all genuine and lasting generosity lies in our own inner fulfillment.

"Not loving yourself is knowing nothing about love."

To understand Paching Hoé's quote, we must explore what self-love truly means and why it is the foundation of our ability to love others. This thought invites introspection on the importance of self-love in our understanding and practice of love in all its forms.

The Essence of Self-Love

Self-love is not a form of narcissism or self-indulgence. It is a profound recognition of one's own worth, an unconditional acceptance of ourselves in entirety, with both strengths and weaknesses. This acceptance and appreciation of ourselves is where true self-love resides. It is the foundation upon which the capacity to love authentically rests, as it teaches the fundamental principles of empathy, compassion, and generosity without expecting anything in return.

Self-Love and the Ability to Love Others

Paching Hoé explains that a lack of self-love limits our ability to understand and express love toward others. If we cannot offer ourselves kindness, patience, and understanding, how can we authentically offer these to someone else? Self-love teaches us to recognize and respond to our own needs and desires, which in turn allows us to better recognize and respect the needs and desires of others.

The Impact of Self-Love on Relationships

Relationships founded on a solid base of self-love are characterized by greater authenticity, openness, and mutual respect. When individuals love and respect themselves, they are less likely to tolerate abusive or neglectful treatment and are more capable of establishing healthy boundaries. Thus, self-love fosters more balanced and enriching relationships where partners can grow together without losing their individual integrity.

The Journey Toward Self-Love

The journey toward self-love can be challenging, especially in a world that often imposes unrealistic standards and expectations. However, this inner journey is essential for a full and fulfilling life. It may involve self-reflection, meditation, therapy, and the daily practice of self-compassion. The aim is to reach a state where self-love is not conditioned by external successes or validation from others, but is a constant presence guiding our thoughts and actions.

Conclusion

Paching Hoé's quote, "Not loving yourself is knowing nothing about love," is a powerful reminder of the importance of self-love in our lives and relationships. It encourages us to recognize that true love begins with ourselves. Cultivating strong self-love is the first step toward the ability to love others authentically and unconditionally, enriching our lives and those around us with a depth and quality of true love.

"I readily admit that I haven't always done what I wanted, but most often what I could."

Paching Hoé invites us to reflect on the consequences of our choices and actions. This quote, imbued with humility, raises important points about accepting our limits, valuing effort, reconciling with ourselves, and the need for flexibility and adaptability in the face of life's uncertainties.

Acceptance of Limits

Recognizing our limits is an essential step that allows us to situate our aspirations within the framework of the real possibilities offered by our environment and personal abilities. This acceptance is not resignation but an act of maturity that encourages us to act with wisdom and discernment, considering the existing constraints.

In the tradition of ancient Egypt, Ptahhotep's maxim, "There is no one who is absolutely competent," encourages us, like Paching Hoé, to accept our personal limits and real capabilities. If even the most learned and competent individuals must acknowledge their shortcomings and continue their learning, so must we. This perspective is liberating: this principle applies to everyone. The challenge lies in persevering in our efforts to progress.

The Value of Effort

The importance of effort lies in recognizing that, even if our actions do not always lead to the desired results, the process itself is significant. It is in the attempt and the commitment that our true success is found, defining success not by the achievement of the goal but by the quality and sincerity of the effort made.

Reconciliation with Ourselves

Reconciliation with ourselves is a call for personal kindness, to recognize and celebrate our accomplishments without excessive harshness for unmet aspirations. This approach fosters a more balanced and forgiving self-image, where successes and failures are seen as integral components of our life journey.

Flexibility and Adaptability
Paching Hoé reminds us of the importance of adaptability and flexibility, essential qualities for navigating a constantly changing world. Learning to adjust our expectations and actions according to circumstances is a key aspect of resilience and personal development.

Conclusion
Paching Hoé invites us to introspect on how we approach our desires and actions. He highlights the necessity of a vision of our life rooted in accepting our limits, valuing our efforts, reconciling with our inner self, and being able to adapt to life's challenges. This philosophy guides us toward a more authentic and fulfilling life, where peace with ourselves becomes the foundation upon which thoughtful and meaningful actions are built.

"The only person it is good to forgive is ourselves."

Paching Hoé emphasizes the importance of forgiving ourselves on the path toward personal fulfillment and inner peace. This principle serves as an invitation to reflection, healing, and self-discovery, encouraging us to fully embrace our humanity with all its imperfections.

Self-Forgiveness: Key to Emotional Liberation
Self-forgiveness transcends the notion of clemency. It is a process of recognizing and accepting our failures, mistakes, and limits. Through this liberating act, we allow ourselves to move beyond the burden of the past, view our experiences as opportunities for growth, and open ourselves to a future filled with authenticity and serenity.

Healing Guilt and Rebuilding Self-Esteem
The feeling of guilt, often rooted in our past mistakes, poisons our existence, preventing us from recognizing our true worth. Forgiving ourselves frees us from this weight, opening us to a positive reconstruction of our self-esteem. It teaches us to see our faults not as indelible marks of failure but as opportunities for growth and learning, thereby strengthening our self-love and respect.

Permission to Fail Without Negative Judgment
By adopting self-forgiveness, we give ourselves permission to fail without inflicting negative judgment. This openness to "failure," seen as a natural part of the process of learning and discovery, fosters a kind approach toward ourselves and encourages resilience and perseverance in the face of life's challenges.

First Step Toward Self-Love and Connection to Unconditional Love
Self-forgiveness is the indispensable first step toward self-love, inviting us to accept and cherish ourselves in our entirety. This intimate journey of self-compassion reflects and connects us to

unconditional love, a universal and benevolent force that transcends human limits and links us to a deeper understanding of the Divine and the spiritual essence of love.

An Ode to Liberation and Personal Growth

Paching Hoé's quote is a guiding light toward the liberation from the chains of our past mistakes and the full embrace of our potential. Self-forgiveness is an inner exploration toward acceptance, renewal, and self-love, laying the foundation for a life filled with peace, personal growth, and true happiness. This profound act of love toward ourselves resonates with lasting healing and harmony, reminding us that far from being a selfish gesture, self-forgiveness is the foundation upon which to build a rich life, at peace with ourselves, and open to future possibilities. It is free of judgments, making this practice pure and transformative.

"Healing is understanding, accepting, rebuilding…"

Paching Hoé invites us on a journey of reclaiming our personal history through understanding, acceptance, and self-reconstruction. This path of healing plunges us into an inner exploration, aiming to align our existence with universal principles. Understanding these fundamental principles and embracing our true essence are crucial for rebuilding our lives on authentic foundations. This method, rooted in reconciliation with our deep nature and the divine dimension, leads us toward a life marked by inner peace, tranquility of mind, and deep harmony with the universe.

Understanding Universal Principles

The first step toward healing, according to Paching Hoé, is understanding. This is not merely acquiring superficial knowledge but delving into the depths of the divine principles that govern our world. This understanding allows us to unravel the threads of our own suffering, identify how our erroneous perceptions of reality and divine will have shaped our beliefs, and thus our experience of pain and conflict.

Conflict with the Creator

Paching Hoé emphasizes that our ignorance or misinterpretation of universal principles places us in a state of conflict, not only with ourselves but also with our Creator. By attributing intentions or responsibilities to God that do not correspond to His true nature, we trap ourselves in an inner struggle, a battle where we seek blame rather than answers. This situation is analogous to the conflicts we may experience with our earthly parents, where misunderstandings and unmet expectations generate tensions and distances. It is interesting to note the similarity highlighted by Paching Hoé between conflict with the Heavenly Father and conflict with "the father."

Acceptance of Universal Principles

Acceptance is the second pillar of healing. Once we begin to understand universal principles, we learn to accept them as the foundation of our existence and growth. This acceptance does not mean resignation, but an openness to the deep wisdom these principles represent. By accepting, we reconcile with the very nature of our being and with our Creator, recognizing that trials and sufferings are opportunities for evolution and strengthening our conscience. This rediscovery gives us a vision of ourselves aligned with the one our Creator has for us. We regain a deep joy, that of being able to grow serenely under the benevolent and loving gaze of God.

Reconciliation with the Creator

Understanding and acceptance naturally lead to reconciliation with the Creator. Paching Hoé teaches us that approaching divine principles, and by extension God, with a clear and conflict-free understanding is crucial for our inner peace. This reconciliation is a healing, not only of our relationship with the divine but also of our relationship with ourselves, as it allows us to see our place in the universe, not as victims of arbitrary circumstances, but as active participants in a greater plan.

Rebuilding on New Foundations

Armed with this understanding, acceptance, and reconciliation, we are in a position to rebuild our lives. This reconstruction is not a simple return to our previous state but a profound transformation that integrates our new understanding of divine principles, our regained peace with the Creator, and our acceptance of ourselves as beings in constant evolution. This new existence is founded on principles of love, understanding, and harmony that protect us from past sufferings and open us to a future filled with possibilities.

Healing: An Act of Love Toward Ourselves

Paching Hoé offers us a spiritually rich vision of healing. By guiding us through the understanding of universal principles, the acceptance of our true nature, the reconciliation with our Creator, and the reconstruction of our lives on renewed foundations, he shows us that healing is a profound act of love toward ourselves. This approach, far from being a solitary journey, is a return to harmony with the world and the Divine, a path that frees us from the chains of ignorance and opens us to the embrace of inner peace and unconditional love.

"Do not judge a situation until you know the end of the story."

Paching Hoé invites us to exercise caution before judging the quality of a situation based solely on its immediate manifestation. He highlights the cyclical and unpredictable nature of life. This teaching urges us to recognize that the true consequences of events in our lives often reveal themselves long after these events occur, transforming our initial understanding and reactions to them.

By insisting that we withhold judgment until we know the end of the story, Paching Hoé leads us to view life as a complex fabric of interconnected events whose true meanings and impacts are only unveiled over time. This perspective encourages us to adopt an attitude of patience and observation, especially in the face of difficult situations that, at first glance, seem purely negative.

This teaching resonates with the concepts of karma and personal transformation. Karma, in its essence, is based on the idea that every action has consequences, which may not be immediately apparent. Paching Hoé reminds us that what we perceive today as a disaster could be the architect of our future happiness, and conversely, what we celebrate as a victory could sow the seeds of future difficulties.

This duality of consequences invites us to embrace a more holistic view of our existence, where the quality of a situation is evaluated not in the immediacy of its effects but in the richness of its long-term outcomes. Such an approach helps us to put our experiences into perspective, appreciate the complexity of life's paths, and cultivate resilience in the face of uncertainty.

Applying this quote to our daily lives requires us to cultivate a keen awareness of the nuances of our experiences, recognizing that behind every trial lies a lesson, and behind every triumph, a challenge to come. It encourages us to live with mindful attention, to value reflection and patience, and to develop the ability to see beyond appearances.

Paching Hoé offers us a key to navigating the complexity of the world with wisdom and balance. He teaches us that the quality of a situation is fully revealed only in its consequences, which may be appreciated long after their occurrence. This understanding urges us to reconsider our relationship with time, adversity, and success, guiding us toward a more thoughtful, resilient, and ultimately more fulfilling life.

Paching Hoé's teaching embraces all facets of the human experience, inviting us to consider every event in our lives, pleasant or unpleasant, as a step toward a deeper understanding of ourselves and the world around us.

"Healing will allow you to transcend your sufferings, in order to realize the most beautiful image of yourself."

A transformative teaching emerges from this quote, illuminating the path to healing as a quest for the most authentic expression of ourselves. This reflection is part of a dialogue with ancient wisdoms, resonating with the richness of psychoanalysis, spirituality, and millennia-old philosophies, particularly Egyptian.

Paching Hoé proposes that we see healing not as mere restoration but as the transcendence of our sufferings. This perspective transforms our relationship to pain: it is no longer an enemy to avoid but a guide to a deeper understanding of our being. Life's trials become catalysts for growth, unique opportunities to forge the "most beautiful image of ourselves." This idea echoes the principles of Jungian psychoanalysis, where confronting our shadow areas unlocks unsuspected potentials of our psyche, revealing our true essence.

Ancient Egyptian wisdom parallels this vision, viewing earthly life as preparation for a higher existence. Sufferings and obstacles are seen as initiatory trials, purifying and refining our soul for its journey toward immortality. This perspective underscores the importance of presenting the gods with a purified version of ourselves, obtained through a life of quest and transformation.

Paching Hoé's quote resonates with the principle that our passage on earth is intrinsically linked to a larger mission, that of contributing to the common good. Personal healing becomes the vehicle for a broader commitment to others, transforming personal trials into opportunities for service and collective harmonization. This idea is embodied in figures like Imhotep, an ancient Egyptian sage who combined knowledge and compassion to transcend individual suffering for the benefit of the collective.

This journey of healing, as suggested by Paching Hoé, is an odyssey toward self-realization, marked not only by challenges but also by revelations about our true nature. It is a call to delve into our darkness to discover the light, to embrace our pains not as burdens but as teachers, opportunities for metamorphosis. This inner transformation, this alchemy of the soul—to borrow from Jung—is the key to unveiling the most beautiful version of ourselves, a being both unique and universally connected, constantly seeking meaning, balance, and harmony.

Paching Hoé's quote, in synergy with ancestral teachings and contemporary reflections, offers us a luminous vision of healing. It reminds us that each moment of suffering is an invitation to grow, to transform, and to reveal the innate splendor of our being, ultimately forging the most beautiful image of ourselves in harmony with the universe.

"He who seeks solutions outside of himself dreams. He who looks within himself awakens."

Paching Hoé distinguishes between two opposing ways of experiencing suffering. On one hand, there is the approach of attributing suffering to external factors, which is the stance of the victim. On the other hand, there is the stance of the warrior, who directs his quest for answers inward and engages in personal actions leading to healing. Adopting one or the other of these stances depends on the degree of self-esteem. For Paching Hoé, the challenge in the healing process is to move from the victim's stance, which endures its situation, to that of the warrior, who initiates concrete changes in his life. This process requires rebuilding sufficient self-esteem and self-confidence to feel capable of taking action.

The victim, as depicted by Paching Hoé, tends to externalize the cause of their suffering, attributing their pain to circumstances or external actions. They experience their situation as an inevitable fate, perceiving themselves as having no influence over change. This attitude creates a sense of powerlessness, reinforcing the idea that change must come from the outside. It is important to understand that this orientation toward external solutions is a direct consequence of diminished self-esteem and self-confidence. This poor self-image complicates the identification of ourselves as an agent of change. It results in weakening us, thereby increasing the difficulty of overcoming suffering.

In contrast, the warrior embraces the idea that they have the ability to transform their perception and reaction to the causes of their suffering. This path requires significant introspection to identify and adjust limiting beliefs and behaviors. Furthermore, the warrior acknowledges their responsibility in preventing or stopping external aggressions. They have sufficiently preserved self-esteem to engage in personal actions leading to healing.

By adopting the warrior's stance, we engage in a dual approach: we transform our internal reaction to suffering while initiating concrete actions to reduce and prevent pain. In doing so, we do not take on the world's burden but recognize that everyone has a role to play in building fairer and more compassionate relationships.

Paching Hoé thus encourages us to realize our potential for healing and transformation, both personally and collectively. By becoming warriors, we embark on a journey of personal development in the face of our challenges and act proactively to protect and improve our world. This approach embodies the essence of resilience and autonomy that Paching Hoé wishes to see us achieve.

In a state of psychological suffering, engaging in a constructive inner dialogue is necessary to untangle emotions and begin a healing journey. Here, I propose a list of questions that integrate the notion of individual responsibility both in our reaction to aggression and in our active commitment to prevent or stop such situations, to help emerge from this state and rebuild:

1. What emotions am I precisely feeling?
—Clearly identifying our emotions for better understanding and management.

2. What contributes to my suffering?
—Detecting the sources to consider suitable solutions.

3. Which elements of this situation are under my control?
—Recognizing our power of action strengthens our sense of agency.

4. What beliefs or thoughts influence my suffering?
—Questioning our perceptions can alleviate the pain felt.

5. Do I feel guilty? If so, where does it come from?

—Understanding and overcoming guilt is essential for moving forward.

6. How do I perceive myself: strong, weak, other?

—Revisiting our self-image can open avenues to strengthen our self-esteem.

7. Is anger present? Is it directed at me or someone else?

—Analyzing anger helps to understand its origin and respond constructively.

8. Do I feel betrayed?

—Identifying feelings of betrayal facilitates dealing with relational ruptures.

9. Do I feel supported and loved?

—Evaluating the support received sheds light on our relational needs.

10. Do I feel an injustice?

—Addressing feelings of injustice can lead to seeking ways to restore balance.

11. What simple actions can I take to feel better?

—Identifying practical well-being actions.

12. To whom can I turn for help?

—Recognizing our support network, whether personal or professional.

13. What am I grateful for?

—Cultivating gratitude to enrich our perspective on life.

14. What self-care measures can I adopt?
—Paying special attention to self-care and physical well-being.

15. What change can I make to avoid experiencing this suffering again?
—Reflecting on life changes to prevent future suffering.

By adding to these reflections the awareness of our role in the prevention and cessation of aggression, we adopt a more holistic approach to healing. This involves not only addressing the roots of our suffering but also taking an active part in creating a safer environment for ourselves and others. Let us not forget that the path to healing is often complex and may benefit from the support of a psychological well-being professional.

"Dare to question your own convictions, instead of assuming your friend is wrong."

Paching Hoé emphasizes the importance of questioning our own convictions rather than assuming the other person is wrong. He invites us to an open-mindedness that transcends personal interactions to touch on the essence of human growth and mutual understanding. This approach is not merely an invitation to be cautious in judgment but a call to an inner revolution, where dialogue with ourselves and others becomes the engine of continuous enrichment.

Within this reflection lies the notion that truth and knowledge are not static entities but dynamic quests, shaped by exchange and questioning. By urging us to doubt our own certainties, Paching Hoé opens us to the possibility of authentic dialogue, not only with others but also with different parts of ourselves. This internal process of questioning and dialogue echoes the teachings of Jungian psychoanalysis, where exploring the unconscious and confronting our shadows are necessary for our psychological development.

In shamanic traditions, the inner journey teaches us that every being we encounter is a mirror of our own reality, offering lessons and perspectives that can only be revealed by an open heart and a mind willing to learn. Thus, Paching Hoé's advice to question our own convictions aligns with this path of knowledge through direct experience and spiritual dialogue.

Philosophy, since ancient times, has valued dialectics as a method of discovering truth. Socrates, through his maieutic method, shows us that the ability to ask the right questions, to ourselves and to others, is key to understanding. Paching Hoé's thought fits into this tradition, emphasizing that questioning our certainties can lead us to deeper and more inclusive truth.

This invitation to self-questioning and open dialogue is also at the heart of modern psychology, which teaches us that our perceptions are often biased by our personal experiences, fears, and desires. Questioning our convictions is therefore essential for developing true empathy, a more nuanced understanding of others, and ultimately, for building more authentic and harmonious relationships.

Ultimately, Paching Hoé's quote is an exhortation to embrace humility, to recognize the limits of our own perspectives, and to welcome the richness that the diversity of viewpoints represents. It is in this creative tension between doubt and certainty, between listening and expressing, that we can truly grow and enrich our understanding of the world. Through this approach, we not only evolve our relationships with others but also contribute to a broader transformation—one where dialogue, openness, and a common quest for truth and harmony prevail over division and conflict.

"Your future lies in choosing to live what you wish for, rather than living what you do not wish for."

Paching Hoé invites us to reflect on the power of our choices and the direction we give to our lives. The quote, rich in psychological, spiritual, and philosophical implications, urges us to rethink our ability to shape our destiny through the decisions we make every day.

At the heart of this reflection is the notion of personal responsibility and inner freedom. The freedom in question here is not the absence of external obstacles but rather the ability to choose our attitude in the face of these obstacles. Psychiatrist and philosopher Viktor Frankl, in his exploration of human resilience, highlighted this form of freedom as the most authentic, asserting that in any circumstance, we have the power to choose our response.

This quote also resonates with psychoanalysis, where an individual's true desires are often masked by layers of social expectations and the injunctions of the superego. Living in accordance with one's true wishes thus requires a process of self-discovery, an inner journey to uncover what truly drives us.

From a spiritual perspective, this statement echoes the law of attraction, which posits that our reality is a reflection of our deepest thoughts and beliefs. Focusing on what we love, rather than what we fear, brings into our existence the conditions and experiences that resonate with those aspirations.

Shamanic traditions, with their intimate understanding of the connections between the individual and the cosmos, emphasize the importance of intention and clear vision in self-realization. The shaman's vision guides not only their own path but also serves as a beacon for the community, illustrating how a life guided by conscious choices impacts far beyond the individual.

In literature, particularly in initiatory novels, this principle is embodied in the hero's journey, where, in the quest for meaning, the hero learns to navigate life's challenges guided by deep choices rather than external circumstances. These stories highlight the inner transformation that accompanies the decision to live according to one's own terms.

To concretely illustrate this idea, consider the story of an individual who chooses to leave a stable but unsatisfying job to pursue a passion for writing. This choice, risky in the eyes of many, embodies the decision to live according to one's wishes. The obstacles encountered along this path are not seen as barriers but as steps in a process of personal growth and self-realization.

In essence, Paching Hoé's quote encourages us to reassess our priorities and redefine our life's path, not to avoid our fears, but to follow our true aspirations. It reminds us that our future is not a series of predestined events but a tapestry we weave with the threads of our decisions, passions, and dreams. Embracing this perspective opens the door to a richer, more authentic, and more fulfilling existence.

"Time spent crying over ourselves is time lost not changing."

Paching Hoé addresses a key aspect of our journey through the complexities of human experience. This seemingly simple quote reveals a profound truth about the relationship between personal transformation and our approach to time, suffering, and the possibility of growth.

At the heart of our exploration lies a duality: on one hand, accepting suffering as an integral part of the human condition, and on the other, the imperative to transcend this pain to initiate meaningful change. Paching Hoé, with empathy and pragmatism, shows us that self-pity paralyzes us and acts as a barrier to our personal and spiritual evolution. Suffering itself is inevitable, but how we respond to this suffering shapes our path toward growth.

In psychoanalysis, this quote resonates with the idea that emotional stagnation, although a natural human reaction, becomes an obstacle to development if we cannot move beyond it. The healing process involves acknowledging and accepting our emotions while mobilizing ourselves to move forward. This attitude reflects the psychological resilience needed to transform pain into a driving force for change.

In spiritual and shamanic traditions, every trial is seen as an opportunity for purification and learning. Stagnating in pain dissipates vital energy that could otherwise be channeled toward personal improvement and service to the community. These moments of pain become rites of passage toward a deeper understanding of our place in the universe.

From a philosophical perspective, Paching Hoé's quote challenges us on the use of our time—this finite resource. How we choose to spend our time reflects our values and aspirations. Viewing self-pity as a waste of time reminds us of the preciousness of each moment and the urgency to act constructively.

The maxim of the Egyptian sage Ptahhotep, "He who wastes time is blameworthy," aligns with this notion. Ptahhotep highlights the importance of wisely managing our time, associating inefficient use of time with both personal loss and ethical failing. This wisdom encourages living consciously and using each moment productively, as individual behavior has personal and social implications. In our modern era, it emphasizes the value of each moment and the impact of our choices on ourselves and our community.

In the realm of initiatory literature, stories of transformation after periods of adversity underscore that trials are crucial steps on the path to self-realization. Heroes discover that how they act in the face of their challenges reveals their true potential. Their actions within trials lead them to find the path to wisdom and peace.

Figures like Frida Kahlo or Nelson Mandela illustrate how personal trials become catalysts for broader change on a community scale. Their journeys invite us to consider our potential to impact the world positively.

In conclusion, Paching Hoé's quote is not only a reminder of the importance of overcoming suffering but also an invitation to recognize and seize the opportunities for change that it presents. It is a call to action, reflection, and transformation, encouraging us not to let the precious time of our lives be lost in immobility but to use it as a lever for continuous growth and fulfillment. This exploration offers a perspective that is not naive but optimistic, deeply rooted in the reality of human experience. Even in our darkest moments, we have the capacity and responsibility to seek the light.

"Stop thinking about what you don't want, what scares you, what you dread. Think about what you want to experience, what you want to achieve, what you want to create."

Paching Hoé emphasizes the transformative power of our thoughts and intentions. Through an exploration of the human mind and its ability to shape our experience of the world, he guides us toward a crucial awareness: creating a reality aligned with what we wish to live requires focusing on our aspirations rather than our fears.

Paching Hoé follows a tradition that values the harmony between thoughts, words, and actions, a principle that resonates across ages and cultures, from ancient Egypt to modern psychology. This harmony, according to him, is not only the foundation of a balanced life but also the driving force of personal and collective transformation.

Gandhi's thought, aligned with that of Paching Hoé, underscores the importance of coherence between our beliefs, thoughts, and actions: "Your beliefs become your thoughts, your thoughts become your words, your words become your actions, your actions become your habits, your habits become your values, your values become your destiny." This quote illustrates the chain of connection that begins with our internal beliefs and ultimately manifests in our external reality. It highlights the importance of integrity and coherence in self-realization and shaping our world.

In this perspective, thinking positively transcends the avoidance of negative thoughts; it is an active practice of creation. By highlighting the importance of nurturing thoughts that reflect our most authentic desires, Paching Hoé raises the significance of inner balance and our harmony with the universe.

This vision aligns with contemporary psychology's concept of cognitive bias, particularly the negativity bias. Cognitive biases are psychological mechanisms that deviate our judgment from rationality. The negativity bias, in particular, is the tendency to give more weight to negative experiences than to positive ones, leading to a pessimistic view of life and affecting our well-being and decisions. By recognizing and understanding these biases, we can work to minimize them, develop more balanced thinking, and improve our ability to evaluate situations more objectively. Paching Hoé invites us to rebalance our perception in favor of a more constructive and optimistic view of our reality.

By consciously shifting our focus from what we fear to what we wish for, we activate a process of neuroplasticity. Our brain reorganizes itself to better align its structures and functions with these new priorities. This transformation goes beyond a mere adjustment of our mindset. It aligns with a universal law of attraction, where the clarity and purity of our intentions actively attract the circumstances that allow the realization of our desires. By cultivating precise and sincere intentions, we facilitate the materialization of our aspirations, creating synergy between our will and the world around us.

Paching Hoé's thought, rooted in faith in the universe and our co-creative capacity, teaches us that aligning our deepest desires with our thoughts and actions is key to achieving our dreams. It is an invitation to live a life that resonates with our highest aspirations, recognizing the innate power we have to transform our internal reality and, by extension, our external reality.

This optimistic perspective, far from being an escape, is an act of faith in the human potential to overcome obstacles and fully realize aspirations. Paching Hoé encourages us to become aware of our inner power and use it constructively to actively shape the reality we desire. It is an ode to practical optimism, inviting us to navigate existence with hope, courage, and renewed creativity.

"You create what you think, so choose to think about what you wish to live."

This quote highlights the capacity of thought to actively shape the reality around us. It embodies a central truth recognized across various disciplines, from psychology to spirituality, emphasizing the role of intention and conscious thought as vectors of change and personal evolution.

The Power of Creative Thought

Our thoughts are not mere internal passengers without impact. They build our world. Creative thought, an active practice of shaping our existence, urges us to align our deepest desires with our daily thoughts. This process transcends mere positivity to embrace a perspective focused on realization and fulfillment. It involves acknowledging our challenges while choosing thoughts that pave the way toward our aspirations.

Choice and Responsibility

The emphasis on individual responsibility in choosing our thoughts is vital. In any situation, we hold the power to choose our mental focus. Practices such as meditation and mindfulness equip us to exercise this choice in an informed manner, guiding us intentionally toward the realization of our aspirations.

Methods of Transformation

Gratitude, visualization, and affirmation of what we want are concrete practices for applying creative thought in our lives. These approaches, through their simplicity, have the potential to radically transform our existence, encouraging us to live fully in the present and align our actions with our most cherished aims.

Spiritual Dimension

The ability to create our reality through thought is presented as a spiritual gift, an invitation to co-create with the universe. This perspective elevates the practice of creative thought, situating it in a quest for meaning and alignment with universal principles, pushing us to consider our aspirations in their capacity to enrich not only our lives but also the world around us.

Thinking Our Reality: A Personal and Collective Commitment

The invitation to "think about what you wish to live" is not merely an encouragement toward optimism but a call to conscious and deliberate action. By intentionally choosing our thoughts, we shape our personal experience and contribute to the creation of a world that reflects our deepest aspirations. This approach is not just a personal commitment to a fulfilling existence; it is also a collective commitment to building a consciously chosen, more harmonious shared reality.

"I have chosen the optimism of youth over the pessimism of reason."

In a society marked by constant challenges, the dichotomy between optimism and pessimism shapes our perception of the world and our interaction with it. The optimism of youth, a burning flame fueled by hope and the aspiration for a better future, contrasts with the pessimism of reason, a dimmer light guided by experience and caution. This inner dialogue, weighing boldness against restraint, lies at the heart of human dynamics, influencing both our personal and collective development.

The optimistic perspective of youth, characterized by a forward momentum, enthusiasm, and a certain carefree attitude, encourages us to dream big and to pursue these dreams with boundless energy. This approach, far from being naive, is based on a deep faith in human potential and the possibilities for improvement and positive change. It urges us to take risks, to experiment, and to learn from our failures without losing our momentum.

On the other hand, the pessimism of reason offers a more measured perspective, enriched by the lessons learned from our experiences and disappointments. This more reflective and analytical vision allows us to assess situations with caution, anticipate obstacles, and carefully plan our next steps. It does not aim to extinguish optimism but to temper it, making it more sustainable and adaptable to the changing realities of our environment.

Often, throughout our lives, we observe a transition from one vision to the other. Youth, with its energy and carefreeness, is naturally optimistic. We dream big, driven by an unwavering faith in a bright future filled with possibilities. As the years pass and experiences accumulate, this initial perspective becomes more tempered and reasonable. Trials and disappointments tend to temper our initial ardor, often leading us to adopt a more cautious and measured view of life.

Paching Hoé invites us to reverse our usual view of these transitions. Instead of seeing these two poles—the optimism of youth and the pessimism of reason—as fundamentally opposed, he invites us to see them as complementary. This transformative approach suggests that, rather than succumbing to increasing pessimism with age, we can choose to nurture and maintain the spark of our youth while enriching it with the wisdom and caution brought by our experiences. By simultaneously embracing these two aspects, we can form a more complete and balanced perspective, capable of effectively guiding us through the complexities and challenges of the modern world.

The harmony between these two perspectives is essential for navigating the complexity of today's world. Adopting an enlightened optimism, which integrates the wisdom and caution of reason, allows us to remain open to possibilities while being aware of challenges. This balanced approach encourages active engagement with the world, where passion and dreams are guided by knowledge and experience.

Applying this principle of balance in our daily lives transforms our way of living, working, and interacting with others. It leads us to embrace bold and exciting careers, to cultivate enriching relationships, and to continue progressing and improving throughout our lives. Ultimately, it invites us to see every challenge not as an obstacle but as an opportunity to demonstrate our resilience, creativity, and capacity to innovate.

Choosing the optimism of youth enlightened by the pessimism of reason is a life choice that allows us to navigate flexibly and effectively through the complexities of the modern world. It is not about denying reality but about choosing to look at it with hope and determination, armed with the wisdom of our experiences. In the end, this polarity does not divide us but enriches us, offering a path to a more complete and meaningful existence.

"Stop looking at how much it costs, and instead consider how much it will yield."

Paching Hoé's quote resonates deeply in an era marked by immediacy and the pursuit of instant gratification. It invites us to adopt a long-term vision. The true return on investment is measured not in terms of material goods but in personal growth, significant contributions to society, and spiritual fulfillment. This approach transcends simple financial analysis to touch on areas as diverse as psychology, spirituality, and philosophy, offering a wealth of interpretations and practical applications.

A Redefinition of Value

At the heart of this quote is the invitation to reconsider our criteria for value. In a world where the price of an object or experience is often perceived as its sole value, Paching Hoé reminds us that true investments are those that bring inner wealth, foster our personal development, and contribute to our long-term well-being. This perspective encourages us to evaluate our choices not only in terms of immediate cost but also in their potential to enrich our lives and the lives of others.

Overcoming Personal Limits

Paching Hoé also highlights the need to overcome our own limits and resistances. The pleasure principle, which drives us to seek immediate gratification, must be tempered by the reality principle, which recognizes the value of short-term sacrifices for long-term gains. This internal dynamic requires deep introspection to identify and overcome our inner resistances, thus allowing us to fully realize our potential.

Investing in Ourselves

In terms of personal development, this quote suggests that the most valuable investments are those we make in ourselves: in our growth, our resilience, and our ability to contribute meaningfully to the world. It reaffirms the importance of perseverance and motivation in pursuing our aims. The most rewarding results are often those that require the most effort and dedication.

The Potential for Growth

The quote resonates with the principles of positive psychology. It encourages a growth mindset, valuing the potential for personal and professional development through challenges. It urges us to see beyond immediate obstacles, recognizing that every effort, every investment of time, energy, or resources carries the promise of a rewarding return, both personally and collectively.

Conclusion

Paching Hoé's quote is a call to look beyond immediate costs and fleeting gratifications to embrace a long-term vision of our existence. It encourages us to invest in what truly matters: our personal growth, our well-being, and our capacity to make a positive difference in the world. This approach, far from being a simple resource management strategy, is a philosophy of life that promotes a richer, more fulfilling, and more meaningful existence.

"The value of our actions is not measured by their form, but by their consequences."

Paching Hoé invites us to reflect on how we measure the quality and impact of our actions. Through a multidisciplinary lens, the quote reveals the hidden dimensions of our actions and highlights the complexity of evaluating them beyond immediate appearances. It challenges our conscience, spirituality, and responsibility, urging us to consider the long-term effects of our choices.

In a world where speed and immediacy often dominate our judgments, this quote encourages us to adopt a more contemplative and thoughtful perspective. It raises fundamental questions about our motivations, the alignment of our actions with our deep values, and the impact of these actions on those around us and the world at large.

Conscience and Introspection

On a psychoanalytic level, this reflection leads us to examine the nature of our desires and how they manifest through our actions. It urges us to distinguish between unconscious motivations and real consequences, offering a powerful tool to better understand and guide our behaviors in a more conscious and intentional manner.

Spirituality and Karma

From a spiritual viewpoint, the quote echoes the principle of karma, reminding us that every act generates consequences that influence our path. This perspective enriches our understanding of action, encouraging us to perform deeds aligned with a positive spiritual imprint and pure intention, highlighting the importance of ethical and thoughtful action.

Impact and Results

In psychology, this quote leads us to consider tangible results as the true measure of an action's effectiveness. It emphasizes the importance of foresight and self-regulation, guiding us toward choices that prioritize beneficial and lasting consequences.

Interconnection and Harmony

Through the lens of shamanic traditions, we are invited to see our actions as extensions of our intentions, interconnected with the entire universe. This perspective reminds us that the quality of an action lies in its ability to create harmony between our needs and those of the community and environment.

Ethics and Consequentialism

Philosophically, the quote challenges us to rethink our criteria for evaluating actions, emphasizing the ethics of responsibility and consequentialism. It urges us to act in ways that ensure the fruits of our actions contribute positively to society and the environment.

Conclusion

Paching Hoé calls us to live a more authentic and meaningful life, where the quality of our actions is appreciated not for their form but for their real contribution to collective well-being. He invites us to a heightened awareness of the consequences of our deeds, guiding us toward enlightened and thoughtful decisions that transcend immediate gratifications in favor of a lasting positive impact. In doing so, the quote offers a moral and spiritual compass for navigating the complexity of the contemporary world, emphasizing individual responsibility in creating a more ethical and harmonious future.

"The truth of who I am is not in what I think or what I say, but in what I do."

Paching Hoé's quote weaves a rich and complex tapestry around human authenticity and integrity. Beyond our thoughts and words, it is our actions that reveal the essence of our being. This universal theme, although ancient, finds particular resonance in our contemporary context, marked by the predominance of image and discourse often disconnected from concrete action.

Authenticity Through Action

Paching Hoé invites us to consider authenticity not as an abstract ideal but as a daily practice. The idea that "I am what I do" is a call to integrity, demanding congruence between our deep values and our actions. This perspective is rooted in a psychoanalytic notion: the unconscious, with its hidden desires and motivations, shapes our actions in a way that is often more faithful than our words can express.

Karma and Selfless Action

Spirituality, illustrated by karma yoga, enriches this reflection. Actions performed without attachment to the results resonate with spiritual authenticity. Every gesture, every choice to act in alignment with our principles, even in the dark or away from the public eye, contributes to our path of personal and spiritual realization.

Congruence as a Path to Authenticity

In psychology, Carl Rogers' work on congruence shows that authenticity manifests when our actions reflect our true self. Congruence refers to the alignment or harmony between a person's internal feelings and their external actions or behavior. When a person is congruent, their actions are in harmony with their internal thoughts and emotions, contributing to a psychologically healthy and authentic life. This perspective involves a commitment to live according to our convictions, even when it is difficult. It establishes authenticity as a practice of courage and resilience.

Action as Expression of Intention in Shamanism

In shamanic traditions, action is considered the manifestation of will and intention. Here, we find another dimension of authenticity. The concrete act becomes a powerful means of effecting change in the spiritual world, emphasizing the profound interconnection between the individual, their actions, and the entire universe.

Self-Construction Through Action

Existentialist philosophy teaches us that it is through our actions that we define ourselves. Our existence shapes our essence. This conception places responsibility on our shoulders: that of choosing our actions to faithfully reflect who we wish to be.

Toward Integrity of Action

Paching Hoé guides us toward an awareness of the centrality of action in expressing authenticity. He prompts us to reflect on how our actions, both great and small, shape our identity and our impact on the world. Recognizing that our deeds are a reflection of who we are, we are invited to adopt an integrity of action. This attitude involves ensuring that our actions are in line with our values and beliefs and acting in an honest and consistent manner—primarily toward ourselves. Practically, having an integrity of action can manifest in simple daily actions, like keeping a promise, or in more complex decisions. Each choice becomes a step toward a more authentic expression of our being.

Exploring authenticity through action provides a framework for personal evaluation and growth. It calls for acting with awareness and intention. It is an invitation to live in a way that respects the depth of our essence and the richness of our potential, in harmony with others and the world around us.

"The quality of our actions reveals the purity of our intentions."

Paching Hoé provides us with a key step toward a life of authenticity and moral responsibility. This universal principle is rooted in introspection and the incessant quest for sincerity in our motivations. It guides us through a journey of personal and interpersonal alignment, where the ethics of intention become the foundation of action.

At the Heart of Authenticity

Paching Hoé's invitation to explore the purity of our intentions leads us toward deep introspection. This inner quest demands that we delve beyond surfaces to touch the core of our desires and motivations. It reveals that authenticity is not a static state but a dynamic process of constant alignment between our deep values and our actions in the world.

The Spiritual Echo of Intentions

In spirituality, pure and aligned intentions are fundamental, as the force of intention transcends the personal realm to touch a universal spiritual dimension. In this light, our intentions become vectors of energy capable of healing, connecting, and harmonizing. The principle of prayer rests on this notion. This perspective reaffirms the idea that intentions invested with purity and benevolence have the power to transform not only our inner world but also the external world.

The Psychological Resonance

Psychoanalysis and modern psychology offer us tools to decipher the layers of our unconscious, allowing us to understand and illuminate the real motivations behind our actions. This process of analyzing and clarifying our intentions leads us to act more congruently, reinforcing our personal integrity and mental health.

A Philosophical and Ethical Perspective

The reflection on intentions also fits into an ethical and philosophical dimension, where the morality of our actions is intrinsically linked to the purity and sincerity of our motivations. This perspective reminds us that beyond the consequences of our actions, the key to a morally rich and ethically solid life lies in the purity of our intentions.

Toward a Daily Practice

Applying this principle in our daily lives engages us in a way of life where every gesture, word, and thought is imbued with conscious and thoughtful intention. By choosing purity in our intentions and aligning our decisions and actions with these intentions, we embrace a conscious and responsible life path. The quality of our presence and interactions becomes a gift to ourselves and to others.

Conclusion

Paching Hoé's quote invites us to reflect on the nature of our motivations, encouraging us to seek, discover, and embody purity in our intentions. In doing so, we embark on a journey of personal and collective transformation. Each action, animated by a conscious intention aligned with our values, becomes an expression of authenticity, benevolence, and harmony. It is with this quest for sincerity in our intentions that we can build a more just, loving, and deeply human world.

"Pure intention is the intention that is aligned with the universal principle."

Paching Hoé invites us to explore the complexity of the intentions that motivate our actions. He emphasizes that intentions aligned with universal principles lead to beneficial outcomes. This reflection fits within an interdisciplinary approach, highlighting the importance of pure intentions beyond the apparent effectiveness of our actions. It underscores the necessity of deep authenticity that resonates with these universal principles, forging a path toward true inner and outer harmony.

Alignment with Universal Principles

For Paching Hoé, pure intentions follow universal principles such as interconnectedness, cause and effect, and balance. These intentions go beyond the mere effectiveness of actions—the immediate and apparent results—seeking to achieve a deeper and more enduring good. Having this intention implies an understanding and consideration of the long-term consequences of our actions, an awareness of their impact on others and the environment, and an approach aimed at supporting harmony and collective well-being.

The Complexity of Intention and Action

Psychoanalysis and spirituality offer enriching perspectives on the nature of intentions. Psychoanalysis shows that our deep motivations are often hidden in our unconscious. In spiritual traditions, intention is the seed from which all actions flow. These approaches highlight the essential role of intention in defining the value and morality of our actions, regardless of their apparent success.

Identifying Our Intentions

The maxim of Ptahotep, "A wise word is more hidden than an emerald, yet it may be found among humble servants grinding the grain," emphasizes that wise words, the outward expression of a pure and authentic intention, are often subtle and hidden. For

Ptahotep, the deepest truths are discovered in simplicity and humility. Understanding our intentions does not rest on observing the external value of our actions but on exploring our hearts.

The Purity of Intention as a Transformative Force
In shamanic practices and philosophy, cultivating pure intentions is a powerful transformative force, capable of guiding our actions toward lasting positive effects. Whether through simple gestures or more complex endeavors, aligning our intentions with values of fairness and benevolence is presented as the foundation of just and harmonious action.

The Resonance of Intention with the Collective
The quote invites us to recognize the real impact of our intentions, not only on our personal journey but also on the fabric of our relationships and society. By seeking truth in our intentions, we engage in a conscious and responsible life path. Each action reflects a deep ethical approach, positively influencing the world around us.

Conclusion
Paching Hoé invites us to reconsider the importance we place on efficiency in our lives. He encourages us to prioritize integrity and purity of intentions. This perspective urges us to cultivate a deep moral and ethical commitment, capable of transcending immediate results. By favoring pure intention, each act becomes an expression of our alignment with universal principles. This worldview leads to a richer and more authentic life, marked by truth and harmony, with ourselves and with the universe.

"Self-confidence increases effectiveness."

Self-confidence is a cornerstone of human existence, influencing our interaction with the world, our aspirations, and our ability to transform our dreams into reality. This inner strength, which emanates from certainty in our abilities and a deep connection with our true essence, drives our personal and professional effectiveness. It is the manifestation of our inner dialogue, nourished by our experience and spiritual understanding. It shapes our behavior, our attitude, and, by extension, our success.

Impact of Self-Confidence on Perseverance and Success

Perseverance is essential for achieving success and personal fulfillment. Ptahotep's maxim, "Activity produces wealth, but it does not last when activity slackens," illustrates the importance of continuous effort, fueled by confidence in our abilities, which is fundamental for both material prosperity and inner and spiritual wealth.

Dynamic Between Patience and Self-Confidence

Self-confidence is directly linked to patience, revealing a dynamic where each nourishes and strengthens the other. Patience, far from being merely the ability to wait, becomes a fertile ground for the growth and flourishing of confidence. This symbiotic relationship between confidence and patience underscores the importance of cultivating both to successfully navigate life's complexities.

Social Influence of Self-Confidence

Self-confidence is also at the heart of our social interactions. It enables us to communicate clearly, share our ideas with conviction, and establish meaningful connections. These social skills, enriched by confidence, enhance our effectiveness in personal and professional spheres, facilitating collaboration, innovation, and conflict resolution.

Leadership and Initiative Through Self-Confidence

In the professional realm, self-confidence is often synonymous with leadership and initiative. It equips individuals to take on responsibilities, inspire others, and tackle ambitious challenges. This assurance has a significant impact on stress management and the ability to overcome obstacles, contributing to quicker recovery and greater resilience.

Cultivating Self-Confidence

Recognizing that self-confidence is not static but dynamic is crucial. This quality is cultivated and developed. Education, life experiences, and past successes play a vital role in building self-confidence. By deliberately confronting doubts and challenges and celebrating our achievements, we strengthen our self-confidence, creating a virtuous cycle of growth and success.

Conclusion

Self-confidence is more than just a personal quality. It reflects our inner dialogue with ourselves and the world around us. It influences our ability to act, interact, and achieve our aims. By cultivating self-confidence, we open the door to a life marked by effectiveness, success, and fulfillment, transforming our view of the world and our place within it.

"Patience is a sign of self-confidence, while impatience indicates uncertainty about ourselves."

Exploring patience and impatience as reflections of self-confidence and personal uncertainty enriches the understanding of our relationship with time, our aspirations, and our self-esteem. This exploration values patience as an essential virtue. This quality becomes a reflection of solid inner confidence, manifesting our ability to face uncertainty and ambiguity with assurance and calm. Conversely, impatience is interpreted as an expression of our doubts and insecurities, revealing an inner struggle regarding the perception of our abilities and self-worth.

In psychoanalysis, patience is linked to the ability to delay gratification, an indicator of psychological maturity and confidence in pursuing long-term goals. This ability to wait reflects good self-esteem and confidence in our interactions with the world. Patience is thus seen as a skill developed from childhood, essential to our well-being and success.

In spiritual and shamanic traditions, patience is a spiritual quality essential to connecting with the Divine and the cosmos. It symbolizes harmony with the cycles of life and faith in the natural order of things, accepting that everything unfolds according to a universal timeline beyond our immediate control.

Philosophy and modern psychology view patience as a manifestation of self-mastery and resilience, necessary for our quest for truth and personal fulfillment. Patience allows us to navigate life's challenges with a more balanced and reflective perspective, providing a solid foundation for personal and spiritual growth.

In our daily lives, considering impatience as a mirror reflecting our uncertainties and doubts about our abilities opens the door to significant personal development. When faced with obstacles or delays, our impatient reactions become signs of concerns about our competence and ability to achieve our aims. Each episode of impatience transforms into an opportunity to examine our fears, confront them, and overcome them. This process, while reducing our tendency toward impatience, strengthens our self-esteem and our ability to face future challenges. Impatience ceases to be a flaw to eradicate, leading to harsh self-criticism and unnecessary guilt, but an opportunity to fortify our self-confidence. Understanding impatience as a manifestation of our internal uncertainties and insecurity transforms it into a lever for personal growth and fulfillment, avoiding the trap of guilt and negative self-judgment.

Paching Hoé's perspective on patience as a reflection of self-confidence and impatience as an indicator of personal uncertainty offers a path to a deeper understanding of our own nature. It encourages us to cultivate patience as an expression of our inner assurance, recognizing that our ability to embrace waiting and persevere in the face of adversity is intrinsically linked to our self-esteem and worldview. This exploration invites us to reassess our relationship with time, to value the process as much as the outcome, and to find in patience a source of strength, wisdom, and fulfillment.

"Have confidence in yourself, and start again."

Paching Hoé provides us with a key to navigate serenely through the turbulence of existence. This quote, at the crossroads of psychoanalysis, spirituality, philosophy, and modern psychology, suggests an approach to life imbued with resilience and personal growth. It exhorts us to perceive self-confidence not as an abstract concept but as the foundation on which rests the ability to rise, transform, and flourish.

Self-Confidence and Resilience
This quote highlights self-confidence as the cornerstone of resilience. Through the lens of psychoanalysis, it invites deep introspection and an inner dialogue aimed at overcoming barriers such as inferiority complexes and irrational fears, thereby unlocking individual growth potential.

The Cycle of Life
Spirituality and shamanic traditions teach us to accept the cycles of life, death, and rebirth as natural stages of our existential journey. "Have confidence in yourself, and start again" resonates as a call to embrace constant renewal, seeing in every end an opportunity for a new beginning.

Philosophy of Action
The quote echoes existentialist philosophy, which values active engagement in constructing one's own life. It underscores the importance of self-confidence in daring to act, in taking initiatives that reflect our authenticity and our will to give meaning to our existence.

Examples and Illustrations
Emblematic figures like Maya Angelou and inspiring myths such as the Phoenix illustrate Paching Hoé's quote. These examples highlight the power of self-confidence and the ability to redefine ourselves in

the face of challenges. Maya Angelou, who transcends painful life experiences into powerful and militant poetry, demonstrates how faith in one's values transforms adversity into opportunities for significant change. Similarly, the Phoenix, regenerating from its ashes, more beautiful and stronger than before, symbolizes continuous rebirth and the importance of overcoming failures in the process of personal growth. Every adversity faced enriches our development, increasing our resilience and fortifying our confidence to confront future challenges. Together, they embody the idea that belief in one's abilities is essential for achieving major accomplishments and leading to profound individual and collective transformation.

Practical Applications

In our daily lives, this invitation to have confidence in ourselves manifests as an openness to experiences, a receptivity to the lessons that each failure brings, and a renewed perseverance toward achieving our dearest aspirations. It encourages us to adopt a life posture where each day is seen as a blank canvas, ready to be painted with the colors of our dreams and actions.

Conclusion

Paching Hoé offers us an enriching and holistic vision of self-confidence as a driving force for resilience and renewal. He invites us to integrate this confidence into the core of our being, to recognize it as an alignment with the cycles of nature, and as a pillar on which to rely to navigate life's challenges. This life philosophy, rooted in self-confidence, proves to be a valuable compass for anyone seeking to surpass themselves and live in harmony with themselves and the world.

"Benevolent authority is order without power."

Paching Hoé's definition of benevolent authority invites us to revisit our understanding of education and leadership, both in the family and professional spheres. His perspective overturns the traditional idea of authority, which often relies on fear and domination, proposing instead a model where love, understanding, and mutual support are at the heart of human relationships.

Benevolent authority, according to Paching Hoé, is based on the idea that true strength lies in the ability to guide without imposing, educate without repressing, and inspire without coercing. It invites parents, educators, and leaders to adopt a more holistic and empathetic approach, where communication and mutual respect are prioritized.

In the family domain, this approach manifests as a parent-child relationship based on dialogue and understanding, while maintaining clear and consistent order and rules. Instead of resorting to guilt or punishment, benevolent authority encourages explaining the reasons behind rules and involving the child in the decision-making process. This method promotes the child's autonomy and self-esteem while ensuring a secure and structured environment where limits are clearly defined but fair. Thus, authority is not overwhelming but rather the foundation upon which the child relies to learn the value of personal discipline and mutual respect.

In the professional sphere, a benevolent leader becomes a source of inspiration for their collaborators. By focusing on motivation and support rather than surveillance and sanction, this form of leadership cultivates a work environment where creativity, engagement, and cooperation can thrive. Employees feel valued and respected, which stimulates their desire to contribute to collective success.

On a psychological and spiritual level, benevolent authority aligns with principles of personal growth and spiritual development. It recognizes that each individual, whether child or adult, seeks meaning and fulfillment. By offering a space where personal freedom and responsibility are encouraged, benevolent authority allows everyone to discover and realize their unique potential.

Paching Hoé's vision of benevolent authority is rooted in ancient traditions. The maxim of Ptahotep, a sage of ancient Egypt, "Let not your authority cause fear; let it give peace of mind. What is taken by force is not given willingly," underscores the effectiveness of leadership that promotes peace, mutual respect, and understanding. This maxim highlights three fundamental principles for exercising moral and effective authority. By avoiding the use of fear as a control method, the leader fosters an environment where individuals feel safe and respected. A peaceful living environment encourages individuals to develop and contribute constructively to society. When people give willingly rather than under duress, they do so with stronger motivation and involvement, benefiting both the individual and the community.

By integrating these ancient wisdoms into modern practices, we see how principles of leadership and authority have evolved while remaining anchored in universal truths about human nature and society. The thoughts of Paching Hoé and Ptahotep remind us that true authority is obtained through trust and respect, rather than coercion and fear.

In summary, Paching Hoé's reflections on benevolent authority invite us to reconsider our interactions with others, whether they are our children, colleagues, or students. They highlight the importance of compassion, empathy, and respect in building healthy and rewarding relationships. By adopting this approach, we can not only enrich our own lives but also contribute to creating a more harmonious and cooperative society where every individual is valued and supported on their path to fulfillment.

"To properly educate and guide our children, we must abandon our fears."

Paching Hoé's reflections on education, centered on the importance of overcoming our fears to effectively guide our children, reveal a profound truth about the role of adults in the development of the next generation. The essence of the quote crystallizes around the idea that to raise resilient, confident, and autonomous individuals, parents and mentors must confront their own anxieties and uncertainties.

Overcoming Fears to Unlock Potential

At the heart of this teaching lies the recognition that our fears, often rooted in our own experiences and insecurities, unconsciously limit our children's development. Psychoanalysis shows how these fears cast shadows on young minds. Spirituality and shamanic traditions emphasize the need to cleanse these apprehensions to maintain harmony and foster an environment conducive to growth.

Education as an Act of Liberation

From a philosophical perspective, education free from fear is not just an act of love but also an act of liberation. It prepares the ground for children to explore, question, and build their own path with courage and determination. This approach encourages autonomy in the child, essential for navigating the complexities of the modern world.

Psychological Impact of Confidence

Modern psychology reinforces this vision, highlighting the transformative impact of a fear-free family climate. By embodying confidence, patience, and resilience, we instill these qualities in our children. Armed with these traits, they develop strong self-esteem and the ability to face challenges with optimism.

Inspiring Examples

Stories of historical and mythological figures, such as Gandhi or Ulysses, who overcame trials through their inner strength, illustrate the power of example. By showing our children how to face adversities with confidence and integrity, we impart invaluable life lessons.

Conclusion

Paching Hoé's teachings invite deep reflection on the act of educating. They remind us that, as parents and educators, our greatest challenge is also our greatest opportunity: to transcend our fears to pave the way for a new generation capable of realizing their full potential. This holistic approach, grounded in psychological, spiritual, and philosophical understanding, offers an enriching perspective on education, emphasizing that true teaching goes beyond the mere transmission of knowledge to touch the very core of the human being.

"Always see your child as someone who does not understand,
rather than as a child who refuses to act."

This quote reveals a profound sensitivity toward both the child and the dynamics of parenting. It invites an empathetic and understanding approach to education, emphasizing the necessity of considering the child as a developing being rather than as someone deliberately resistant.

Let's examine the choice of words. The use of the verb "see" evokes a conscious and deliberate action, suggesting a posture of attentive and thoughtful observation. By using the adverb "always," Paching Hoé highlights the importance of this attitude in all interactions with the child, indicating that it is a fundamental principle in education.

The opposition between "does not understand" and "refuses to act" is significant. Paching Hoé highlights the distinction between a child's inability to grasp an instruction or situation and a deliberate resistance to obey. This nuance is essential to avoid making hasty judgments about the child's behavior and to foster a benevolent and constructive approach.

This quote also reveals a deep understanding of child psychology. By perceiving the child as someone who does not understand, Paching Hoé implicitly acknowledges the natural limits of their cognitive and emotional development. He invites parents and educators to adjust their expectations according to the child's developmental stage and to adopt teaching and communication methods appropriate to their level of understanding.

In the parent-child relationship, this quote highlights the importance of empathetic communication. By prioritizing understanding over reprimand, parents create a climate of trust and mutual respect within the family. This attitude encourages the child to express their needs and emotions openly and constructively, thereby strengthening the emotional bond between family members.

To illustrate this quote in daily life, imagine a parent asking their child to tidy their room. Instead of immediately assuming that the child refuses to clean up out of laziness or disobedience, the parent could take the time to clearly explain their expectations, the reasons for the request, and the benefits for the child of living in a tidy room. By adopting a patient and empathetic approach, the parent helps the child understand the importance of tidiness and encourages them to cooperate willingly.

In conclusion, Paching Hoé offers valuable advice for parents and educators, emphasizing the importance of patience, empathy, and understanding in child rearing. By adopting this perspective, adults foster a healthy and nurturing family environment conducive to the child's flourishing and harmonious development.

"We don't punish our child; we teach them through example, repetition, and patience."

Paching Hoé's educational philosophy presents a rich and nuanced vision for guiding a child toward his fulfillment. This perspective, marked by the abandonment of punitive methods in favor of teaching through example, repetition, and patience, highlights a renewed approach to education based on empathy, respect, and encouragement for personal growth.

The Power of Exemplarity

Paching Hoé reminds us that exemplarity is the foundation of all virtuous education. The child, an attentive observer of their environment, naturally imitates the behaviors of the authority figures around them. Being a model of kindness, respect, and patience teaches these values far more effectively to the child than any words or punishments. By embodying the principles we wish to transmit, we guide the child toward their authentic integration.

The Value of Repetition

Far from being mere redundancy, repetition is identified by Paching Hoé as an essential pillar in anchoring learning. It allows a progressive familiarization with the desired concepts and behaviors, facilitating their assimilation. This method recognizes that learning is an evolving process, requiring time and repeated exposure, and invites a patient and persevering education.

Patience, a Primary Virtue

Patience is elevated to the rank of a primary virtue, indispensable for the harmonious development of the child. It demonstrates an understanding and respect for each child's individual pace, encouraging a safe learning environment where the child can explore, fail, and progress without fear of judgment or reprimand. This quality is essential for building a trusting and supportive relationship between the child and the adult.

A Holistic Approach

Paching Hoé embraces a holistic approach to education. He highlights the necessity of a transformation in educational methods, favoring encouragement and benevolent support. This vision emphasizes the importance of shaping conscious, responsible, and kind human beings capable of contributing positively to society.

Paching Hoé's teaching transcends simple pedagogical directives, touching the very heart of human relationships. He invites us to rethink our way of interacting with the younger generation, encouraging us to cultivate values of empathy, patience, and love. His approach offers a framework not only for the child's growth but also for the personal development of each educator, shaping a future where education is a vector of positive transformation for the individual and the community.

"The secret is a wall that we build to do the opposite of what we teach."

In the quest for authenticity and integrity, Paching Hoé invites us to reflect on the dissonance between our words and actions. This quote confronts us with the duality of our nature. Secrets act as partitions, separating our proclaimed ideals from our actual behaviors. They reveal an internal tension between our aspiration to integrity and the reality of our contradictions.

The notion of a secret, described as a wall erected, prompts us to explore the deep reasons that motivate us to conceal certain truths or act in contradiction to our teachings. This wall symbolizes not only a barrier between ourselves and others but also raises the question of the fragmentation of our identity: a public face, conforming to expectations and social norms, and a private side, where unspoken desires and actions inconsistent with the projected image reside.

Beyond critiquing hypocrisy, this reflection highlights the complexities of human existence. Each individual struggles to harmonize their multiple facets in a world where appearances exert pressure. The quote encourages us to recognize the importance of congruence between our values and our actions. Integrity is not merely a matter of transparency but also a commitment to ourselves and to others.

This perspective resonates with spiritual and shamanic traditions, where truth and authenticity are seen as fundamental to inner balance and healing. In this view, secrets represent obstacles to personal development, shadows that hinder the free flow of vital energy and the full realization of ourselves.

From a psychological standpoint, concealment and the discordance between teachings and practices generate cognitive dissonance, a source of stress and discomfort. This inner tension, if unrecognized, harms our well-being and our relationships, creating an increasing gap between an idealized self-image and our true nature.

Philosophically, the quote leads us to ponder the value of authenticity and transparency in our interactions with others and with ourselves. It questions the inherent challenges in the quest for a life lived in harmony with our dearest principles.

In summary, Paching Hoé encourages us to tear down the walls of secrecy to embrace an existence where authenticity and integrity guide our steps. It is in the acceptance of our complexity and in striving for coherence between our convictions and actions that we find the key to a fulfilled and authentic life.

"The Master's pure intention is to help us, not to talk about
himself."

Paching Hoé immerses us in an exploration of the true essence of teaching and mentorship. He illuminates the obscure paths of power dynamics and hidden intentions in human relationships. This quote unveils the contrast between the genuine desire to help and the pitfalls of ego and domination.

Teaching, in its noblest expression, transcends the mere transmission of knowledge. It is an act of selfless love, where the master, far from seeking to impose their greatness, becomes the bridge facilitating the student's growth. The teacher helps the student explore and realize their abilities, guiding and supporting their journey toward profound personal development. This approach demonstrates a significant understanding of otherness, where the teacher acts not as a mirror reflecting their own light but as a window open to the infinite potential of the learner.

However, this ideal pedagogical relationship is often threatened by figures of power who, under the guise of teaching, seek to assert their own superiority. These pseudo-mentors, misled by their desire for control and admiration, hinder rather than promote the path to knowledge and wisdom. The distinction between these two figures highlights the importance of discerning the true intentions behind the teacher's actions.

Spirituality and shamanic traditions, with their emphasis on authenticity and connection, offer enriching perspectives on this theme. They remind us that truth and spiritual enlightenment can only be achieved in a space of mutual respect and freedom, far from the chains of ego and manipulation.

Modern psychology, echoing these ancient wisdoms, highlights the deleterious effects of cognitive dissonance caused by teaching that does not align with actions. This inner conflict, a source of stress and anxiety, undermines self-confidence and trust in others, eroding the foundations of our psychological well-being.

Paching Hoé challenges us on the importance of integrity and humility in any helping or teaching relationship. He invites us to seek and embody the figure of the true Master, whose sole ambition is to illuminate the path of others, without shadow or detour. In doing so, he encourages us to become sources of pure light, guiding others not toward ourselves but toward their own self-discovery and understanding of the universe.

In this quest for authentic and benevolent mentorship, we are all called to become masters in our own way, sharing our wisdom and support with those we encounter. By transcending the traps of ego and cultivating a pure intention to help, we contribute to building a more harmonious world, where everyone is both a teacher and a learner in the grand cycle of life.

"The Master says to his student: 'When I look at you, I see my past; when you look at me, you see your future'."

Paching Hoé sheds unexpected light on the master-student relationship, revealing a shared journey through the time and space of learning. This quote plunges us into the contemplation of the continuity of life. Every interaction becomes a thread woven into the fabric of human existence, connecting the past, present, and future in an eternal cycle of transmission and transformation.

This thought rests on an understanding of the cyclical nature of existence. It highlights the beauty of passing wisdom between generations. It underscores the importance of humility and empathy in the master-student relationship. The master, seeing their past in the eyes of the student, is reminded of their own journey marked by trials, mistakes, but also victories. Their gaze illustrates the vulnerability and growth that characterize the path to wisdom.

The student, on the other hand, sees in the master's eyes the promise of a future where the possibilities for personal growth and fulfillment are infinite. This glimpse into the future is a source of inspiration and guidance. The master's example shows that despite obstacles and challenges, the path to spiritual maturity and knowledge is paved with valuable lessons and shared wisdom.

This mutual recognition creates a profound bond between the master and the student, each seeing in the other a reflection of their potential and achievements. This interaction emphasizes the shared responsibility in the learning journey, where each plays an essential role in the other's growth.

Beyond the traditional educational context, this quote resonates with the principles of spiritual and shamanic traditions, which value the transmission of sacred knowledge and universal truths. It evokes how esoteric knowledge and keys to understanding the world are passed from master to disciple. True teaching transcends mere communication of information, becoming a sharing of experiences and worldviews.

In the grand continuum of time, we are all, both masters and students, engaged in a perpetual process of discovery, learning, and teaching. This quote encourages us to recognize and honor our place in this cycle, to embrace our role in the unbroken chain of human wisdom. It reminds us of the importance of living with intention, opening our hearts and minds to constant learning and generously sharing our knowledge and experience.

Ultimately, Paching Hoé offers a profound and enriching reflection on the relationship between teachers and students, the intergenerational transmission of knowledge, and our role in weaving the collective history of humanity. He invites us to contemplate with humility and gratitude the bonds that unite us through time, urging us to recognize the value of each shared lesson and every hope for the future that we offer and receive.

Conclusion

Here we are at the end of the first volume on Consciousness. This concluding point is, in reality, just an opening toward a broader and deeply transformative adventure.

Preparation for Awakening

In this first book, we explored how our vision of ourselves, others, and the world influences our existence. The teachings presented prepare us for the next phase of spiritual evolution: Awakening. Transitioning from consciousness to awakening requires actively reflecting on ourselves, our thoughts, and our beliefs, and deciding to change what distances us from our true nature and deepest aspirations.

Personal transformation, a recurring theme in Paching Hoé's teachings, is a journey that is both complex and enriching. This metamorphosis is not limited to a mere change in behavior or a superficial modification of our habits. It is an inner revolution, a rediscovery of who we are and what we aspire to become. Paching Hoé guides us on this path filled with challenges, offering the necessary tools to navigate the sometimes tumultuous waters of our psyche.

The Complexity of the Transformation Path

This journey begins with the awareness of our thoughts and beliefs, a complex process. Our thought patterns are deeply rooted, based on past experiences, cultural influences, and social conditioning. Paching Hoé invites us to examine these beliefs critically, question their validity, and recognize their impact on our lives. He emphasizes that our reality is shaped by the lens through which we choose to see the world. Recognizing and questioning our habitual thought patterns is essential for making real changes in our lives.

The Courage and Perseverance Needed

Changing these thought patterns and beliefs requires courage and determination. It is often more comfortable to remain within the familiar framework of our habits, even if they are destructive or limiting. Paching Hoé reminds us that healing and transformation are acts of bravery, requiring us not only to confront our fears but also to commit to a process of self-reconstruction that can be long and demanding. The notion of healing runs through his quotes like a red thread, reminding us that pain and trials are opportunities for growth and transformation.

Commitment to Ourselves

This journey requires constant commitment to ourselves. Personal transformation requires more than occasional efforts. It requires a daily practice, continuous attention to our thoughts and actions, and the will to develop thoughts aligned with our values and aspirations. It is a commitment to live authentically and consciously. For each person, the journey is marked by their own timeline, with its challenges and revelations. Patience and perseverance are indispensable virtues. Significant and lasting changes require time, constant effort, and faith in the transformation process. Despite the obstacles and moments of doubt, perseverance bears fruit.

By guiding us through the labyrinth of our psyche, Paching Hoé offers us the key to unlocking our potential for healing and growth. He invites us to recognize and embrace our complexity, to face our fears, and to transform our challenges into stepping stones toward a richer and more fulfilling existence. This path leads to true freedom and self-realization, opening the way to a life created freely and consciously, in line with our values and deepest aspirations.

An Odyssey in Three Volumes

Our journey does not end with the conclusion of this book. We are, in fact, at the threshold of a literary and spiritual odyssey, addressing the three phases of spiritual evolution: Consciousness, Awakening, and Wholeness. Each stage will be explored in a dedicated volume. This format aims to create a rich dialogue between ancestral wisdom and contemporary application, between the universal and the personal.

Consciousness: The Foundation of the Journey
—We have just traversed the first volume, "Consciousness," which lays the foundation of Paching Hoé's thought. This book is designed as an introduction to the principles that illuminate the path toward increased self-awareness and understanding of the world.

Awakening: The Transformation
—The next book will delve into the phase of Awakening, with a volume focused on Paching Hoé's reflections on personal transformation.

Wholeness: Achieved Harmony
—Finally, the series will conclude with the volume on Wholeness, where Paching Hoé will teach us how to achieve inner harmony and peace in our lives.

As we embark on this adventure, we are invited to explore the inner territories of our being, reflect on our journey, and discover ways to transform our lives concretely and sustainably.

Looking Up

As we turn the last page of this first volume, it is time to lift our gaze to the horizon, to the infinite possibilities that our journey of transformation holds. The conclusion of this book is not a farewell, but an invitation to continue walking, exploring, and growing, armed with the precious teachings we have discovered together.

Continuous Commitment to Awakening

The path to awakening and self-realization is endless. Each day offers new opportunities to confront the aspects of our lives we may have neglected or avoided, to face and transcend our fears, and to make decisions that bring us closer to our true essence. Paching Hoé does not impart concepts for mere contemplation but calls to action, urging us to fully embrace the potential of our transformation.

Inspiration for the Future

Looking toward the future, I invite us to see each challenge, each moment of doubt, and each success as essential steps on our own path of growth. May the teachings shared here serve as inspiration and guidance as we navigate the complexities of life, seeking to create a future filled with meaning, joy, and inner peace.

A Call to Consciously Create Our Existence

This book is a vibrant call for each of us to take charge of our destiny, to become the conscious architects of our own lives. It is an invitation to live fully, realize our aspirations, and contribute meaningfully to the world around us. Paching Hoé encourages us to view each moment of our existence as an opportunity to choose, create, and celebrate life in all its richness and complexity.

Paching Hoé reminds us that we possess within us the strength, the tools, and the light necessary to overcome difficulties, to heal, and to progress. As we continue on our path, let us remember that we are never alone. The teachings of Paching Hoé, the stories of those who came before us, and our own inner light are there to guide us. Let us walk confidently toward the future, with open hearts and awakened minds, ready to embrace all that life has to offer with joy, awareness, and responsibility.

Glossary

Congruence (Carl Rogers)

Congruence, according to psychologist Carl Rogers, is the state of coherence between a person's thoughts, feelings, and behaviors. A congruent person is authentic and transparent, acting in alignment with their internal values and emotions. This authenticity is essential in interpersonal relationships and psychotherapy, as it allows for open and honest communication. In therapy, a congruent therapist creates a safe and empathetic environment, facilitating personal growth and the development of self-esteem in the patient.

Ego

The ego is the part of our mind that perceives itself as a distinct "I" separate from others. It is the source of our sense of personal identity and influences how we see ourselves and behave in the world. A healthy ego is necessary for self-realization, as it provides the confidence and motivation needed to pursue our goals, make decisions, and assert ourselves. A lack of ego leads to low self-confidence, loss of identity, excessive dependence on others, and a tendency toward passivity and conformity. An overly dominant ego distances us from our true nature and connection with others. Paching Hoé teaches the need to restore the ego to its rightful place, not to eliminate it.

Evolution of Consciousness

The evolution of consciousness is the process by which a person expands and deepens their understanding of themselves and the world. It is a progression from limited awareness to a more expansive and enlightened consciousness. The aim of this evolution is to achieve greater clarity, wisdom, and inner alignment, enabling the individual to live more authentically and harmoniously with their environment and deep values.

For Paching Hoé, the evolution of consciousness is the hidden purpose of our life experience. He believes that the divine plan is oriented toward our consciousness's evolution and that everything created promotes this development. According to him, every experience, challenge, and interaction in our lives is designed to help us grow and elevate our level of consciousness, guiding us toward a deeper understanding of ourselves and the universe.

Healing

Healing is the process of restoring physical, mental, emotional, or spiritual health. It involves not only eliminating or reducing symptoms of illness but also restoring the individual's overall well-being and balance. Healing can be facilitated by medical interventions, psychological therapies, spiritual practices, and lifestyle changes. It is often perceived as a journey toward wholeness and inner harmony, integrating the body, mind, and soul. For Paching Hoé, the process of healing involves understanding, accepting, and rebuilding.

Higher Self, Higher Spirit, Soul

The Higher Self is often understood as a more elevated and enlightened version of ourselves. It is the aspect of our identity that transcends the concerns and limitations of the ego, aspiring to higher ideals of truth, compassion, and wisdom. The Higher Self is guided by spiritual values and seeks to align our life with our true essence.

The Higher Spirit refers to an advanced state of consciousness and refined intellectual and spiritual capacity. It is the aspect of our mind capable of perceiving deeper realities and understanding universal truths. The Higher Spirit transcends ordinary thoughts and daily concerns, aiming for a more holistic and enlightened understanding of life.

The Soul is often considered the eternal and immaterial essence of our being. It is the source of our vitality, deep emotions, and true identity. The soul is seen as immortal and connected to a larger spiritual dimension. It is the seat of our intuition, moral conscience, and aspiration to transcendence. Paching Hoé uses the terms "Higher Self" and "Higher Spirit" interchangeably with "soul," highlighting its different aspects and dimensions.

Holistic

The term "holistic" refers to an approach that considers a system in its entirety rather than focusing on its individual parts. In psychology and medicine, a holistic approach takes into account the whole person—body, mind, and emotions—to understand health and well-being. This means evaluating how different aspects of a person's life (physical, mental, emotional, social, and spiritual) interact and influence each other. The aim is to promote overall balance and harmony rather than treating isolated symptoms.

Impermanence (Buddhism)

Impermanence, or "anicca" in Pali, is a fundamental concept in Buddhism that emphasizes that everything in life is transient and constantly changing. Nothing is permanent, whether material objects, emotions, thoughts, or situations. Understanding and accepting impermanence helps reduce attachment and suffering, as it makes us realize that everything, including difficulties and pleasures, is ephemeral. This awareness fosters an attitude of detachment and inner peace, allowing for a more balanced and serene life.

Individuation (Jung)

Individuation is the process by which a person becomes a unique and distinct being, fully realizing their potential and integrating different aspects of their personality. Carl Jung saw individuation as a path to self-realization, where the unconscious and conscious come together to create inner harmony.

Instinct

Instinct is an innate and automatic behavior that manifests without learning or conscious thought. It is a natural response to what happens around us, biologically inherited and observed in all members of a species. For example, babies have the sucking instinct, allowing them to feed from birth. Instinct guides us in crucial survival situations, such as seeking food or avoiding danger, and often operates outside of our conscious control.

Interdependence

Interdependence is a key concept in psychology and philosophy that emphasizes that all beings and phenomena are interconnected and mutually influence each other's existence. In Buddhism, this principle is called "pratītyasamutpāda," or "dependent origination," and explains that nothing exists in isolation; everything is connected and co-dependent. In daily life, interdependence manifests in human relationships, ecosystems, and social and economic systems. Recognizing interdependence fosters a deeper understanding of our place in the world, encourages compassion and respect for others, and underscores the importance of harmony and cooperation for collective well-being.

Intuition

Intuition is the ability to understand or know something immediately without needing conscious reasoning. It is a spontaneous feeling or thought that seems to arise from nowhere. Carl Jung considered intuition a psychological function that allows us to perceive hidden possibilities and truths. It works in the background of our mind, connecting experiences and knowledge in often mysterious but deeply meaningful ways. According to Paching Hoé, intuition is guidance from our soul.

Middle Way (Buddhism)
The Middle Way in Buddhism is the balanced path between the extremes of excessive indulgence and severe austerity. Taught by the Buddha, it advocates living with moderation and wisdom, avoiding excesses and deprivations. This approach leads to serenity and spiritual awakening by cultivating attitudes of compassion, patience, and understanding while following the Noble Eightfold Path, which guides toward an ethical, meditative, and wise life. According to Paching Hoé, the Middle Way is synonymous with balance. Anything excessive in the spiritual approach nourishes the ego and does not last, leading to a drop in self-esteem. Buddha recommends a reasonable action that respects well-being, integrating the notion of time. Paching Hoé constantly emphasizes that "everything is a matter of time." This means that patience and respecting one's own pace are essential for authentic and lasting spiritual growth.

Psyche
The psyche is a term that refers to all aspects of the human mind and emotions. It encompasses thoughts, feelings, dreams, memories, and desires. In Carl Jung's analytical psychology, the psyche includes both the conscious and unconscious, with elements such as the ego, shadow, animus/anima, and self. The psyche is seen as a dynamic system in constant interaction, influenced by internal and external forces, and playing a crucial role in forming our identity and behavior.

Psychiatry
Psychiatry is a branch of medicine focused on diagnosing, treating, and preventing mental, emotional, and behavioral disorders. Psychiatrists are specialized doctors who can prescribe medications,

conduct therapies, and intervene medically to treat conditions like depression, anxiety, schizophrenia, and bipolar disorder. Their approach often combines biological, psychological, and social methods.

Psychoanalysis
Psychoanalysis is a therapeutic approach and personality theory founded by Sigmund Freud. It studies the unconscious, dreams, repressed memories, and internal conflicts to understand and treat mental disorders. Psychoanalysis uses techniques like free association, dream analysis, and exploration of past experiences to bring unconscious elements to consciousness, promoting healing and self-understanding.

Psychology
Psychology is the scientific study of behavior and mental processes. It covers a wide range of areas, including cognition, development, emotions, social relationships, and mental health. Psychologists can work in various settings, such as research, teaching, health services, and organizations. Unlike psychiatrists, psychologists generally do not prescribe medications but use therapy and counseling techniques to help individuals understand and modify their behaviors and thoughts.

Relationship Between the Unconscious and the Conscious
The unconscious and the conscious are two aspects of our mind that constantly interact. The unconscious contains thoughts, memories, desires, and experiences that are not immediately accessible to our consciousness but strongly influence our behaviors and emotions. The conscious, on the other hand, is the part of our mind that actively processes information we are currently aware of.

The interaction between these two parts of the mind is essential for our mental well-being. For example, when unconscious content becomes conscious, we can better understand our deep motivations and resolve internal conflicts, promoting personal growth and greater inner harmony.

Shadow (Jung)

The shadow, according to Carl Jung, is the part of our personality that we prefer to hide or ignore. It contains aspects of ourselves that we consider negative or unacceptable, such as repressed fears, desires, or behaviors. Recognizing and integrating our shadow is essential for personal growth, as it allows us to understand and accept all facets of our being, leading to a more balanced and authentic life.

Spirituality

Spirituality is a dimension of human existence that involves the search for meaning, connection, and transcendence. It often goes beyond religious doctrines and manifests in a personal quest for understanding and harmony with ourselves. It aims to nourish the soul, develop deeper awareness, and live in accordance with spiritual values such as love, peace, and truth.

Paching Hoé emphasizes that spirituality is individual, while religion is collective. For him, the spiritual approach is defined by: "I seek, I doubt." In contrast, religion is: "I know, I am right, you are wrong... this is not negotiable." This approach fosters excessive ego and a sense of superiority, whereas the other promotes the evolution of consciousness.

Suffering

In psychology, suffering is an unpleasant and subjective experience that can be physical, emotional, or mental. It often results from situations of stress, trauma, loss, or internal conflict. Emotional suffering can manifest as sadness, anxiety, anger, or despair. It is considered a natural response to life's difficulties but can become problematic if it is intense or prolonged, affecting mental well-being and quality of life. For Paching Hoé, suffering is the main driver of consciousness evolution.

Superego (Freud)

The superego is a concept in psychoanalysis, introduced by Sigmund Freud, representing the part of our mind where internalized moral norms and values reside. It acts as a kind of conscience, guiding our behaviors according to learned rules and standards, often from parents and society. The superego seeks to control instinctive and biological impulses to conform to these moral norms. It plays a crucial role in shaping character and moral sense but can also lead to feelings of guilt or shame when behaviors do not meet internal expectations.

Unconscious

The unconscious is a part of our mind that contains thoughts, memories, and desires we are not directly aware of. It influences our behaviors and emotions without our conscious awareness. According to Carl Jung, the unconscious consists of two levels: the personal unconscious, which contains individual experiences and memories, and the collective unconscious, which holds universal archetypes shared by all humanity.

Wholeness (Egypt, Buddhism)

Ancient Egypt:

In ancient Egypt, wholeness is often linked to harmony and balance between the body, mind, and cosmos. The Egyptians believed that living in Ma'at (truth, justice, harmony) allowed one to achieve a state of wholeness and inner peace. This concept was central to a balanced life and a serene transition to the afterlife.

Buddhism:

In Buddhism, wholeness is achieved through the realization of Nirvana, a state of liberation from the cycle of suffering and desires. The practice of meditation, mindfulness, and detachment from worldly attachments leads to a state of inner peace, compassion, and wisdom. Wholeness is thus seen as spiritual awakening and union with the true nature of the mind.

Your Feedback Matters and Contributes to the Success of Our Book!

Leave a comment on Amazon to share your reading experience.

Your opinions are valuable to us, and we are grateful for your support.

Every comment helps us improve our work and allows other readers to discover our book.

Thank you for your support,

Paching Hoé

To contact the authors:

Marie Chieze

wordsoftheshaman@protonmail.com

Design: Paching Hoé & Marie Chieze
Composition and layout: Marie Chieze, June 2024

Made in the USA
Columbia, SC
19 June 2024

37008113R00120